Praise for *Smart Answers to Tough Questions*

"*Smart Answers* is a terrific book, one sorely needed by classroom teachers, administrators, and parents who have been bombarded with exaggerations, half-truths, and outright lies about scientifically based reading instruction over the past seven years. It is rare to find such a combination of practicality and scholarship in one place. Not only can readers go directly to the questions they need answers for, they can select the answer level appropriate for the given audience."

> —Joanne Yatvin, author of *English-Only Teachers in Mixed-Language Classrooms: A Survival Guide* and 2006-07 president of NCTE

"Once again, Elaine Garan has written an invaluable resource for educators caught in the crossfire between pseudo-science and best pedagogical practice for students. The easy-to-read format includes suggestions for effective teaching and learning, as well as 'bottom-line' answers to frequently asked questions about literacy instruction, English language learners, standards, and accountability. Elaine's answers to each question are validated with evidence or 'proofs' from a variety of relevant research, including the National Reading Panel. No educator should be without this book!"

> —Priscilla Gutierrez, outreach specialist, New Mexico School for the Deaf

"When teachers are being told their best practices are not 'research based,' Elaine Garan has proven otherwise with quotes from the *National Reading Panel Report* and other scientifically based research. Teachers will now be able to support their child-centered, not program-driven, instruction with the very research others have misused. This book is a gift every teacher should own."

> —Libby Correll, literacy specialist and leader of a Twelve-County Literacy Team in the Seattle area

"Not only do the answers in this jewel of a book help teachers, Elaine's insights can aid parent groups and teacher leaders who are concerned about school practices as well. When teachers, parents, and leaders come to the classroom door with a desire to support children with effective instruction, children learn. Elaine's book will pave the way."

> —Nancy Akhavan, principal of Pinedale Elementary School, California, and author of *How to Align Literacy Instruction and Standards* and *Accelerated Vocabulary Instruction*

"Not only does this book provide answers to tough questions, but it also draws a detailed picture of what research-based practices look like in the classroom. I see this as a guidebook for best practices in literacy education, as well as a resource for talking with parents about these issues."

> —Joy Widmann, fourth-grade teacher, Louisburg, North Carolina

"Elaine's 'smart answers' evoke a renewed respect for teachers, helping everyone to understand why highly educated professional minds and child-centered hearts get better results than scripts, programs, and political mandates."

> —Ardith D. Cole, literacy consultant and author of *When Reading Begins* and *Knee to Knee, Eye to Eye: Circling in on Comprehension*

"*Smart Answers to Tough Questions* is a multifaceted look at the role relevant research should play in professional conversations with colleagues, parents, and educational administration. . . . An exceptional textbook for a university-level methods and research course."

> —Penny Batchelor, K-1 teacher, Visalia, California

"This book is a tool I shall keep at my fingertips to answer those tough questions parents and colleagues ask. After reading it, I feel like a smarter teacher."

> —Mary Wilson, teacher, Port Townsend, Washington

Smart Answers

TO TOUGH QUESTIONS

*What to Say When You're Asked About
Fluency, Phonics, Grammar, Vocabulary,
SSR, Tests, Support for ELLs, and More*

Elaine Garan

■ SCHOLASTIC

NEW YORK ◆ TORONTO ◆ LONDON ◆ AUCKLAND ◆ SYDNEY
MEXICO CITY ◆ NEW DELHI ◆ HONG KONG ◆ BUENOS AIRES

Dedication

Much of who I am, both professionally and as a person, I owe to my dearest friend and mentor, Ardie Cole. I could not have written this book without her.

Cover and Interior Designer: Jorge J. Namerow
Acquiring Editor: Lois Bridges
Production Editor: Raymond Coutu
Copy Editor: Shea Dean
ISBN-13: 978-0-439-02443-3
ISBN-10: 0-439-02443-9
Copyright © 2007 by Elaine Garan

3 4 5 6 7 8 9 10   40   12 11 10 09

Acknowledgments

I owe a great deal to many people without whom I could not have completed this book. Right at the top of the list is Lois Bridges, who listened to my pleas and agreed to continue as my editor. Lois has been unwavering in her integrity, her passion for good teaching, and, of course, her support of me as a writer.

This is a book that answers questions teachers are asked. I'm indebted to all the teachers who took time out of their busy schedules to send me those questions. These include Ginger Weincek, Joy Widmann, Olga Reynolds, and Heather Wall. I'm also grateful to Diane Frame, Nancy Barth, Tiffany Taylor, and Mary and Ken Wilson for their ongoing support and for being such caring and smart teachers.

Laura Alamillo was a big help in shaping the section on ELLs. My son, Chris Baker, proved himself to be a meticulous and supportive reader, and I value his suggestions. I'm also grateful to my daughter, Holly Shakya, for her insights from the perspective of a parent. Thanks to them all.

No matter what topic I was addressing in this book, it seemed that all roads led to Steve Krashen. I worked on SSR and there he was. When I looked for information on ELLs, the Accelerated Reader program, phonics, and phonemic awareness, there was Steve, tirelessly working on behalf of kids and teachers. It's impossible to express my gratitude for his generosity and passion.

I owe a lot to Alfie Kohn's work on testing and homework. His books and articles are cited throughout, and I hope my mention of them will inspire readers to go right to the source. Jim Trelease is a true icon in the field of reading, and I can't thank him enough for his exuberant, lifetime dedication to the truth that kids need to be read to and that real literature is a good thing in schools. I used his Web site for information and inspiration throughout the writing of this book.

I'm grateful to the administrators of California State University, Fresno, because they have never questioned my work or tried to hold me back. Without their support, I'm not sure I could have written this. These include President John Welty and Provost Jerri Echeverria. Right at the top of the list, though, is Dean Paul Beare, who encouraged me every step of the way. Without the commitment of these administrators to academic freedom, I could not have accomplished all that I have. Thanks also to my department chair, Judith Neal, an amazing professional who has supported me from the day I set foot on campus in 1998. I thank her for all she's done for me and for her unwavering commitment to Reading Recovery and her fight to make sure that all kids get only the best.

I owe a great deal to the late Steven Stahl for his contributions to the field of reading, but particularly for his work on fluency and his clarification and reframing of the findings of the National Reading Panel in *The Voice of Evidence in Reading Research*. His work was invaluable to me in the writing of this book and I wish I'd thanked him when he was alive.

Last but not least, I must thank my parents, Elizabeth and Eugene Garan. Both are second-generation Americans whose parents spoke little or no English. Both worked so hard and sacrificed so much to make sure that my brothers and I had every advantage. My parents gave me many gifts, but the one I treasure the most is their integrity and the model they set for us. They are both still writing letters to the editor, and neither will let an injustice or a lie slide by without at least trying to fight the wrong and maybe even right the wrong.

Thanks to you all.

Contents

Section V: Fluency

Tough Questions About:

Section VI: Writing

Tough Questions About:

Section VII: English Language Learners

Tough Questions About:

Section VIII: Standards, Accountability, and High-Stakes Testing

Tough Questions About:

Section IX: Summary/What Is the Role of the Teacher in Teaching? 156

Index 158

Dear Teachers,

These are exciting and challenging times in education and for us as teachers. Did you know, for example, that a recent survey conducted by *USA Today* showed that teachers are in the top tier of people who have won the trust of the public? But there's more. Another poll, conducted by a prominent education journal, revealed a related finding: While those who responded to the survey believed that education in general is in trouble, they nevertheless had faith in their children's teachers and believed they were doing a good job.

So why this dichotomy within the public's perceptions of education? What does it boil down to? It seems apparent that the public, parents in particular, make a distinction between the two: you, the teacher—*the individual* who personally cares for their children—and *the institution* of education.

Challenges, Accountability, and Standards

Parents trust us and they have more faith in us than they do in the system in which we as teachers must function. They care what we say and they care what we think. As a result we have enormous power and we can effect positive change in our classrooms *if* we have the tools to articulate our instructional choices within that larger system. And to do that, we need to speak the language of the system.

Today, of course, the two constant refrains we hear are "accountability" and "scientifically based" instruction. Prominent columnist and advocate for educational reform Brent Staples notes in the July 19, 2006, *New York Times*:

> "*The instructional techniques for helping . . . . children are well documented in federally backed research and have been available in various forms from specialized tutors and private schools for more than 50 years. Even so, few public schools actually use the best practices*" (p. A18).

Clearly, as Staples reminds us, we, as teachers and as representatives of the system of education, have a responsibility to be knowledgeable about the federal research that frames public policy—particularly when we are faced with huge numbers of struggling readers and English language learners in our classrooms. We must be prepared to account for our actions and defend them as being evidence-based and scientifically sound instructional methods.

However, many of us do not have the time or the background to defend our practices to parents, administrators, and even the media, with the appropriate scientific research. The purpose of this book is to help you articulate the answers to tough questions about your classroom practices, from a scientific-research perspective. Although the answers I provide are stated in plain English—in language that you can use when you speak with parents or even when you write letters to the editor in response to one of the many challenges leveled at teachers on a daily basis—they are based on scientific research. They are almost always from the federal government's own studies and, therefore, are unassailable.

This book will give you the tools not only to defend your classroom practices but to be proactive in your teaching as well. That is, you can use it to infuse innovative but scientifically based methods into your classrooms. If we have the right tools and we can speak the right language, we can respond to challenges as highly qualified professionals. As such, we can—and *should*—participate in the decisions that affect the students in our care. This book will help you achieve those goals.

How to Use This Book

This book is organized into categories of issues in literacy. The tough questions were contributed by real teachers from all over the country. They are questions that are frequently asked by parents and raised in the media but are difficult to answer for many teachers who don't have a background in research.

Each section follows the same format:

◆ "The Tough Question": One frequently asked by parents or that we see raised in newspaper articles

- "Your Bottom-Line Answer": An explanation that you can use in workshops or when explaining your practices to parents or administrators

- "Something for You to Think and Talk About": A section that raises issues that extend and refine the bottom-line answer—a good source of activities for group work in professional development workshops

- "The Proof": A categorized, annotated synthesis of the relevant research, stripped of research jargon, including many powerful quotes that you can download for professional development workshops, newsletters, and university courses

In other words, you can rely on "Your Bottom-Line Answer" to articulate your response and then use "The Proof" section to bolster your argument by citing some background information on the studies and researchers. I hope you will keep this book on your desk as a handbook and a reference tool.

A Note to Literacy Coaches, Workshop Providers, and Administrators

This book is set up for use in professional development workshops. In fact, it is organized in such a way that you can turn to a topic and find the outline and content clearly laid out. Important quotes are set off on the page and are downloadable from www.Scholastic.com/Garan for use on overheads and PowerPoint slides. As such, the book can save you a lot of time and trouble scrambling for research to back up the practical methods you are presenting. In most instances, I provide background information on the studies, as well as links to federally sanctioned studies that frame education policy, which will help you present credible evidence. As you give workshops and presentations, you can intelligently and convincingly articulate the importance of the studies and researchers you cite and their role in shaping federal education policy.

In addition, the "Something for You to Think and Talk About" section provides provocative questions and talking points for group discussions. I hope you will use it for that purpose during workshops or in discussions with your peers, or just for your own self-reflection.

My purpose in writing this book was to help you maintain a balance between the need for accountability, scientifically based professional development, and good teaching. The information here will help teachers to become an articulate force for good practice and a part of the decision-making process in their classrooms—all of it based on scientific research, most of it from the federal government, most of it the very research designed to frame education policy.

There's a good chance that you'll be surprised at what the science *really* says! Remember, parents and the public trust you. You have the power to advocate for and to defend what is best for students. I hope this book will help you do just that.

Elaine Garan

Note: For ease in downloading, each quote is accompanied by its relevant references and background information, so you don't have to go hunting through prior sections to find them. Therefore, some references and background information appear in more than one section. In addition, I placed quotation marks around block quotes, even though that is not formal APA style. I did this to emphasize the quotes and make them easier for you to use in presentations and newsletters.

Reading

1
Reading Aloud to Students

The Tough Question

"There are just so many hours in the school day, and my son is under a lot of pressure to do better on the big tests. However, you spend precious time reading out loud to the class. While this is very nice and entertaining for the students, wouldn't they be better off if you spent that time teaching them to read?"

Your Bottom-Line Answer

You Can Say: When I read aloud to my class, I *am* teaching reading. In fact, a large study showed that the greatest predictor of later success in reading is the number of stories children listen to. So naturally, I am using that research to inform my instruction. Research also overwhelmingly shows that *reading aloud to students teaches reading skills in a variety of areas.* Here's a list of the many skills that research confirms I am teaching when I read aloud:

- Students develop new vocabulary just from listening to stories. This is especially important for my English language learners and for students who need vocabulary development.

- Listening to books helps students (and adults for that matter) learn about places and situations that are not directly related to their limited world experiences. It also exposes students to information and ideas that they may not yet have the ability to read about on their own. Listening to books makes them more knowledgeable, and that knowledge translates to all areas of the curriculum.

- I also read aloud to help students, especially English language learners, hear the difference between conversational language (the informal speech we use when speaking to one another) and the more structured, sophisticated language of print. Understanding this distinction strengthens reading comprehension as well as writing skills, since the language we typically use in writing is more structured than the language we use in casual conversation. I want my students to be aware of that distinction.

- Reading aloud also helps children understand the conventions of print. It helps them see how print works. That's one of the reasons I sometimes use big books and point to the words as I read. While I do teach those conventions directly, reading aloud helps your child experience them "in action."

- Research shows reading aloud helps with decoding—sounding out words.

- Reading aloud doesn't threaten my struggling readers. By including them in the activity of listening to stories, I can inspire in them a love of books and make them want to learn to read on their own.

- Reading aloud helps students develop their listening comprehension, a very important skill. They don't do this when they are reading on their own.

◆ Reading aloud helps establish a warm, caring relationship between my students and me. It is a shared experience. I'm not grading them or in any way judging them during our read-aloud time. We come to the stories together. In contrast, independent reading and skills practice are isolated acts.

In view of all of the evidence-based advantages, I would be remiss if I did *not* read aloud to my students.

Something for You to Think and Talk About

I don't believe I've ever seen a handbook or a list of suggestions for parents about how they can help their children at home that didn't include reading aloud with them, especially for younger children. Also, I don't believe I've heard the many benefits of reading aloud *explained* to parents at all, much less from a research perspective. Instead, I've heard vague explanations such as "It helps them with their reading." What's more, I think a lot of teachers are not aware of the strong research base and the galaxy of skills we teach when we read aloud. What I'd like you to think about is this: Why not strengthen your position and your credibility by citing the specific benefits of and the research base for reading aloud when you speak with parents or administrators? You have enough information here in "The Proof" section to be specific and even to name the researchers when you defend your practice.

One more observation that's worth considering: reading aloud isn't a long, arduous, time-consuming activity, nor should it be. Even though your day is really crowded with required curriculum, you can find a few minutes at the beginning of the day, after lunch, or at the end of the day to read to students. It's soothing. It quiets them down. It engages them in a way that our intensely visual society has robbed them of. Instead of a strobe light of images from video games, television, and billboards, students learn to linger, to listen, to connect, and to make their own pictures in their heads.

If you doubt this, think of how compelling books on tape are for us as adults. If you've ever listened to a book on tape in your car, I'd be willing to bet that if you reached your destination at a crucial point in the story, you drove around the block or sat in the car draining your battery until you found out what happened next. You probably recall with affection listening to stories your parents told or sitting around a campfire spinning tales. Probably, many parents have had that experience too, and we can use that as a touchstone for explaining why we read aloud to students. We can give children those experiences that are fast fading away in today's society with its intense, constant parade of visual images. If we don't, where else in their world will students experience the pleasure of just listening to and being hooked on a really good story?

Don't forget that not all children have the same level of literacy in their homes. Not all of them have had the advantage of listening to stories and following along as their parents read to them. We have a responsibility to fill that experiential gap. We need to level the playing field for those children who struggle more than their literature-savvy peers. So in addition to the overwhelming support from researchers, reading aloud just makes good sense.

The Proof

1. Reading aloud to children helps them acquire vocabulary and experience events beyond the limitations of their own worlds, thus making them more knowledgeable.

Here you can cite the strong evidence from a study by literacy expert Warwick Elley, as well as the research funded by the federal government and on which federal education policy is based. Elley's work is significant for the following reasons:

◆ It was an experimental study that used a medical research model. That is, some children were "treated"—read to—while others (the control groups) were not treated (not read to). Both groups were pre- and post-tested on their vocabulary acquisition, and their scores were then compared. Because it used an experimental *medical model*, Elley's study met the government's rigorous criteria—the gold standard for research.

◆ It showed that even without any explanation of vocabulary, the children who listened to stories learned statistically significantly more vocabulary than those who did not. With some teacher discussion of vocabulary, the children learned *even more*.
This makes sense when we stop and think about it. When children learn to talk, we don't give them dictionary definitions of abstract words such as *hungry* or *scared* or even of concrete nouns such as *milk* or *cookie*. They learn vocabulary though experience, through the rich, lived context that gives words their value and utility. What listening to stories does is provide experience and context that many children might not ordinarily have.

Smart Answers to Tough Questions

What's more, students learn the meanings of words from the context—the way the words are used in the surrounding text. This is a vital comprehension skill that we may not even be aware of using. When we as adults are reading for pleasure, most of us do not carry around a dictionary. We glean the meanings of unknown words from the context of what we are reading. Students need to learn this skill, and reading aloud to them helps them do so. Remember, too, that vocabulary is an *essential* component of comprehension.

◆ Elley's study is what's known as a *landmark*, or *seminal*, study. It is widely cited and respected in the field of research. It is worth mentioning Elley's name when you discuss vocabulary acquisition as a benefit of reading aloud to students.

To Literacy Coaches, Workshop Providers, and Administrators

The background I've provided on Elley's study is important because all research is not created equal. Providing some of that background can give your workshop presentations credence. The following is a quote from Elley's study that you might put on an overhead or into a PowerPoint presentation:

"The findings support the assumption that . . . children can learn new vocabulary incidentally from having illustrated storybooks read to them. As in previous studies, teachers' additional explanations of unknown words as they are encountered can more than double vocabulary gains. Furthermore, the evidence from these studies indicates that students who start out with less vocabulary knowledge gain at least as much from the readings as the other students, and that learning is relatively permanent . . . . Several identifiable features in the stories appear to account for [the learning]: the frequency of the occurrence of the word in the story, the helpfulness of the context, and the frequency of the word in pictorial representation" (p. 184).

Elley, W. (1989). Vocabulary acquisition from listening to stories.
Reading Research Quarterly, 24, 174 – 187.

2. **Active participation (conversations and student-initiated questions during read-alouds) further bolsters vocabulary acquisition because students are actively constructing and applying vocabulary in an important way. They are translating the vocabulary they acquired through listening to yet another context—*oral language.***

Reading aloud to students provides that engagement and rich context. Best of all, *you have federally sanctioned, scientific research to bolster your case.* Here are some quotes from the federal government's *Report of the National Reading Panel:*

"The nature of the interaction (emphasizing active participation) during storybook readings may also have an impact on learning" (p. 4 – 21).

"Studies found that student-initiated talk or active participation was important" (p. 4 – 21).

"Active learning is best" (p. 4 – 26).

> National Institute of Child Health and Human Development. (2000). *The report of the National Reading Panel: Report of the subgroups (comprehension).* Washington, DC: U.S. Government Printing Office. The report can be accessed and obtained free at www.nationalreadingpanel.org

The following quote is from National Reading Panel member Michael Kamil in *The Voice of Evidence in Reading Research,* written to explain the findings of the National Reading Panel for teachers:

"The context in which a word is learned is critical. Lists are generally less effective than connected text for learning most vocabulary . . . . Students learn words better if they are actively engaged in the task of inferring vocabulary meanings from context rather than simply being given the definition" (p. 218).

> Kamil, M. (2004). Vocabulary and comprehension instruction: Summary and implications of the National Reading Panel findings. In P. McCardle & V. Chhabra (Eds.), *The voice of evidence in reading research* (pp. 213 – 234). Baltimore, MD: Brookes Publishing.

3. In order to attain high levels of literacy, children should be immersed in literature-rich environments.

The following quote is by federally approved researcher Catherine Snow, a highly respected researcher out of Harvard University:

"The superordinate prevention strategies identified by the committee were: (1) ensuring that all children have access to excellent, language- and literacy-rich school environments" (p. 245).

Snow, C. E. (2000). Brookings papers on education policy: Comment
by Catherine Snow on the federal bilingual education program
(pp. 244 – 255). Washington, DC: Brookings Institute Press.

4. Reading aloud to students helps them develop their listening comprehension, a vital skill that is being lost in today's world of visual images.

Here, you can cite Elley again and also Dickinson and Smith, who showed the long-term benefits of reading aloud on low-income children's reading comprehension *and* vocabulary.

Elley, W. (1989). Vocabulary acquisition from listening to stories. *Reading
Research Quarterly, 24,* 174 – 187.

Dickinson, D. K., & Smith, M. W. (1994). Long-term effects of preschool
teachers' book readings on low-income children's vocabulary and story
comprehension. *Reading Research Quarterly, 29,* 105 – 122.

5. Research shows that reading aloud to children is a powerful predictor of reading success. When children are read to, they learn many important language skills and concepts about print in a warm and nurturing low-stress environment. Reading aloud to children has a positive effect on kids' brain development. Those children who have not been read to are at a disadvantage. Teachers need to provide the experiential background of stories through read-alouds to level the playing field and to help narrow the achievement gap

A Final Thought

Reading aloud to children is not your entire reading program! You need to emphasize that you still do direct skills instruction. However, by reading aloud to your students, you lay a meaningful foundation and establish a context for the skills you will most certainly teach.

To Literacy Coaches, Workshop Providers, and Administrators

What follows is a vital quote you can use in professional development workshops. Teachers, the quote is excellent for use in newsletters to explain your practice because it's by G. Reid Lyon, who was the head of the National Institute of Child Health and Human Development and was known as George W. Bush's "reading czar" and a major influence on NCLB legislation:

"One of the things some of our studies do is look at the interactions that occur between moms and dads and kids. When you look at professors working with their kids from birth onward, they're reading to those kids from day one, typically. They are not only reading, but as they read . . . . they're pointing out the letters and the sounds. They're getting the kids to see the relationships between letters and sounds and vocabulary and concepts; they're extending language . . . . What they're doing is building not only knowledge of language and print and how all of that goes together, but they're building brain. We can see kids who don't have these interactions, and they show us brain development substantially different from kids who do have these interactions . . . . They are kids from disadvantaged families whose parents are working too hard to interact in the ways I just described, who may themselves not read, where there may not be books in the home."

Lyon, G. R. (2003). Converging evidence, reading research: What it takes to read. Interview with David Boulton for Children of the Code. Available at www.childrenofthecode.org/interviews/lyon.htm#Personal

You can also name names and studies! The power of the research base includes long-term studies, and here you have powerful researchers you can cite. Gordon Wells did an extensive, longitudinal study that showed the greatest predictor of reading ability in children was the number of stories they were read! Along the same lines, Dolores Durkin did research involving more than two thousand first graders in two separate studies. She found that the greatest predictor of reading success—learning to read early and easily—was whether or not children had been read to. What these two dynamic and very powerful studies show is the bottom line of the other research we cited here: the combined effect of increased vocabulary, comprehension, and print conventions all come together to produce stronger readers. Furthermore, the benefits are long term.

Durkin, D. (1966). *Children who read early: Two longitudinal studies.* New York: Teachers College Press.

Wells, G. (1986). *The meaning makers: Children learning language and using language to learn.* Portsmouth, NH: Heinemann.

2

Round-Robin Reading

The Tough Question

"When I was learning to read, I remember being in reading groups. We sat in a circle and took turns reading. I notice you don't do that. Why isn't my daughter practicing her reading the way that worked for me?"

Your Bottom-Line Answer

You Can Say: New findings from large federal research studies show that "round-robin" reading— having students take turns reading small sections of text—is actually counterproductive and is not a good use of my class time. Here are the reasons I no longer do round-robin reading:

♦ There is strong scientific evidence that the only student who's actually paying attention to the text is the one who's reading. The others are generally off task. And as soon as a student finishes her turn, *she* stops paying attention, too.

♦ It forces struggling readers to perform—and probably fail—in front of their peers. This embarrasses them and makes them hate reading. I want all my students, including struggling readers, to love reading, instead of squirming with dread and embarrassment.

♦ Research shows that students find round-robin reading boring.

♦ The student who is reading can be so concerned about sounding good that even she isn't thinking about what she's reading. Round-robin reading "wastes instructional time," according to the latest federal research. Therefore, I've stopped using it. Instead, I use effective, evidence-based alternatives.

Something for You to Think and Talk About

The purpose of round-robin reading, of course, is to give children time for "eyes on text." However, the research overwhelmingly shows that regardless of where students' eyes are, their minds are probably somewhere else. I recall doing round-robin reading from first grade all the way through high school, where even at that level we went around the room, each reading a paragraph from our social studies book. I vividly remember counting the number of paragraphs from the person currently reading up to where we'd be in the text when it came to my turn and practicing my paragraph so I wouldn't sound bad in front of the class. I could not have told you what I read, much less what the people before and after me read. I also recall how nervous I felt. In fact, to this day, while I can speak to large audiences easily, my voice trembles and I grow extremely nervous when I am actually reading a portion of any text aloud. I can't help but think that my years of round-robin torture are responsible. Perhaps you've had similar experiences.

In the next sections, I provide evidence-based alternatives to round-robin reading that engage, rather than bore and embarrass, students. We no longer need to rely on ineffective, outdated methods. Scientific research can enlighten and enliven our teaching.

The Proof

I divided the proof here into two parts. First are the federally funded research documents that synthesized the research on round-robin reading. The second section lists the studies that *The Voice of Evidence in Reading Research* and *The Report of the National Reading Panel* used to draw their conclusions. Note: both were sponsored by the National Institute of Child Health and Human Development and used to drive federal education policy.

The following quote is from Steven Stahl's section of the federally approved book *The Voice of Evidence in Reading Research*, written to explain the findings of the National Reading Panel:

"Round-robin reading forces low-performing children to perform publicly [and] it is boring . . . . I believe that the major problem is that it wastes instructional time . . . . In classes where round-robin reading predominated, children read an average of 6 minutes per day with low-achieving readers often reading less than 2 minutes per day" (p. 190).

> Stahl, S. (2004). What do we know about fluency? Findings of the National Reading Panel. In P. McCardle & V. Chhabra (Eds.), *The voice of evidence in reading research* (pp. 187 – 211). Baltimore, MD: Brookes Publishing.

This next quote is from the federal government's own NRP report:

"These procedures [round-robin reading] have been criticized as boring, anxiety provoking, disruptive of fluency, and a waste of instructional time and their use has been found to have little or no relationship to gains in reading achievement. It is evident that with round-robin procedures students receive little actual practice in reading because no child is allowed to read for very long" (p. 3 – 11).

National Institute of Child Health and Human Development. (2000). *The report of the National Reading Panel: Report of the subgroups (fluency)*. Washington, DC: U.S. Government Printing Office. The report can be accessed and obtained free at www.nationalreadingpanel.org

A Final Thought

It's not enough to say why you *don't* use a particular instructional method such as round-robin reading. You need to be able to articulate what methods you *do* use and why. The next sections will help you with that. You might also want to take a look at Michael F. Opitz and Timothy Rasinski's nifty guide, *Good-Bye Round Robin: 25 Effective Oral Reading Practices* (Heinemann, 1998). It's just 112 pages but offers up one helpful alternative to round-robin reading after another. Read this little book and you'll never need to lean on round robin again.

3

Big Books and Enlarged Text

The Tough Question

"I see these gigantic books in your classroom. We never had these kinds of books when I was in school. What are they used for? What are you teaching with them?"

Your Bottom-Line Answer

You Can Say: Research shows that the greatest predictor of reading success is whether or not children have been read to at home. By using big books and other forms of enlarged texts through an assisted, shared reading approach, I'm imitating that experience. By using enlarged texts, pointing to the words, and having the children read along with me, I'm teaching the following skills:

- ◆ **Directionality**—Students learn that we read from left to right and make a return sweep when we come to the end of a line because I'm pointing to the words, or sweeping under them, as we all read together. This directionality is obvious to us, but some students don't necessarily understand this concept. You realize this when you look at their early efforts at writing—the words are all over the page. Remember, too, that some students may have had first-language experiences in languages other than English. For example, Chinese and Hebrew are not written or read from left to right. Having students watch as I sweep my finger or a pointer across an enlarged text shows them how the alphabetic principle operates in English.

- ◆ **The alphabetic principle**—Students learn that the sounds of language are represented by letters, that those letters form words, that words form sentences, and that these building blocks all come together to make meaning. Because I go back into the story after we've read it and directly teach phonics sounds and challenging words, students see the alphabetic principle in action, in a way that makes sense to them.

- ◆ **Speech to print** (one spoken word equals one written word)—Your child learns this because I point to the words in simple, short text as I read. As I do this, I am careful not to fall into the trap of reading one word at a time instead of fluent, meaningful phrases. After we've read the story, I go back into the text and directly teach skills such as phonics, and we all discuss new words and vocabulary.

- ◆ **Print carries a message**—Your child learns that print is not just a bunch of squiggles on the page. He learns that reading is supposed to make sense. This is not as obvious as you might imagine. Research shows that some students who haven't been read to a lot at home really don't understand that reading is about understanding the message of text. Often they think it's about sounding out words or completing workbook pages.

- ◆ **Fluency and prosody**—Your child also learns and practices *fluency* because I am reading with expression and she and the rest of the class are reading right along with me. Students pick up on the rhythm of written language. This is especially important for students whose first language is not English. Listen to someone speaking French or Spanish and you'll hear different rhythms and intonations. We call the unique rhythms and phrasing of language *prosody*.

- ◆ **Comprehension**—As the class and I are sharing the text, we talk about the story and make connections to the students' own lives and to other books that they've read. I have the children "turn to the person next to you" to discuss ideas in the story. This gives them a chance to actually construct language, to use and practice new vocabulary, and to ask what they wonder about. In this way I help students remain actively engaged throughout the assisted shared reading as they practice higher-level critical-thinking skills. Furthermore, students are getting multiple exposures to vocabulary in context as research recommends.

Research shows that all of these skills are essential for reading and that shared reading followed by group discussion helps to build them. Big books and enlarged print are the canvas I use to teach many print and comprehension skills, as the research tells me I should. What's more, shared reading using big books and other forms of enlarged print helps struggling readers read without being embarrassed. It builds their confidence. My job is to make sure all students succeed.

Something for You to Think and Talk About

Just as some teachers don't know all the research-based reasons for reading aloud to students (see Question 1), some also aren't aware of the reasons for using big books. I think it's important to be familiar with the layout and text in big books.

For example, *There Was an Old Lady Who Swallowed a Fly* by Simms Taback is a beautifully illustrated, very clever rendition of the song. On each page, the old lady's stomach has a hole in it so students can see the next creature she'll swallow. I observed one of my student teachers using the big book version of the book with a group of kids. It has a predictable, cumulative story structure, so that's a plus in terms of teaching reading skills. And the hole in each page makes it great for helping students make predictions. But the text contains a variety of fonts and the print does not move from left to right. It's scattered all over the page, in columns, nestled in corners and in quote balloons coming out of animals' mouths.

Nevertheless, my student dutifully swept her pointer across the text as she read it, here, there, and everywhere. For those students who still didn't understand directionality, I'm not sure that particular book used in that particular way was appropriate. I think we need to be careful that what we're doing is helping and not confusing students early in the reading process.

I've noticed, too, that when big books became popular, some publishers thought the whole point of them was that the books were big. I've seen big books with so much text on the page that the print was virtually invisible to students. Nevertheless, my student teachers still dutifully pointed to the words that no one could see.

I'm not suggesting that teachers shouldn't use books that do not have a clear, traditional text format. But if we keep the purpose in mind, if we think about what exactly it is that we want to stress with enlarged text, then not all big books serve the same instructional purpose. In fact, some, such as *There Was an Old Lady Who Swallowed a Fly,* are probably better as read-alouds that just happen to have wonderful, big pictures.

Here's something else to think about: The use of shared reading using enlarged texts does not have to be limited to commercial big books. You can make your own big books using butcher paper as a class project, perhaps as a follow-up activity to a story you've shared together.

You can also put poems and songs on chart paper. The words to songs offer an added dimension to supporting readers because the rhythm, rhyme, and tune actually help students to predict the next word. Music is a wonderful way to calm and focus kids as you transition from one activity to another. Just put on a tape, or start singing yourself, and point to the words on chart paper. The class will join you.

Consider writing a daily letter to the class on chart paper, asking the students to help you sound out the words as you write. Keep it real. Use real language and real events from your own life. I used to write about my cats. The class came to know them and looked forward to their latest adventures. You can then use that class letter to have students highlight punctuation and phonics patterns. Throw in some challenging vocabulary as you write. After you've written and read that letter together, type it up and let students read to one another and then take the letter home for more *repeated readings.* Thus, students get multiple exposures to vocabulary in a research-proven instructional method.

One more way to create your own shared text is the *language experience approach.* Have students dictate a story or some news from their own lives. You can do this with individual students or as a group activity. Write exactly what students dictate on chart paper or on an overhead and have them help sound out the words. Because students are participating in the writing, they are directly practicing phonics using their own words and they are actively engaged, as research tells us they should be. Their own words then become the text that they use to practice reading—just make copies of the text and give them to the class after you've all written it. Students are then engaged in repeated readings of the text and they can take the copies home to reread and show off a bit for their parents. This is a kinder, gentler, and more family-friendly type of homework than a lot of what gets sent home. You can also encourage parents to do language experience with their children's dictated stories at home. I would add that language experience is also a powerful teaching tool for older students who are struggling.

Look at it this way: We wouldn't think of teaching math skills without showing students or, better yet, helping them discover how to work the problems. Why would we teach reading without demonstrating the process and helping students discover how print works?

Through shared reading using enlarged text, children are learning how print looks and how reading sounds. They are learning how it all comes together to make sense. Without that final, essential piece of the puzzle, all the other reading skills are useless.

Therefore, shared reading is not a just-for-fun, rather vague activity for motivating students toward reading for pleasure. It is direct instruction. When you share reading using enlarged text, you're saying to your students, "This is what reading looks like. This is what reading sounds like. This is how letters and words come together to make sense. Come along and read with me. You'll see!" That's not just common sense. It's what research proves.

The Proof

1. **Shared reading experiences between children and adults are a powerful predictor of reading success for children. Such experiences provide them with concepts about print and lay the groundwork for many reading skills.**

You can cite the two large, seminal longitudinal studies (by Dolores Durkin and Gordon Wells, below) that support reading aloud to children. Both are cited in *The Voice of Evidence in Reading Research* by members of and contributors to the federal government's National Reading Panel report. The big book shared reading experience replicates the sharing of text children and parents experience at home.

Durkin, D. (1966). *Children who read early: Two longitudinal studies.* New York: Teachers College Press.

Wells, G. (1986). *The meaning makers: Children learning language and using language to learn.* Portsmouth, NH: Heinemann.

2. Shared reading significantly improves students' writing ability as well as their reading ability.

Here you can cite the huge series of very influential studies by Warwick Elley and Francis Mangubhai. They were known as the "book flood" studies because the researchers flooded dozens of classrooms with high-interest books and trained teachers in shared reading instruction. The results were remarkable. Not only did the thousands of students in the study—all of whom were learning English as a second language, by the way—improve in reading, they also improved in writing! You'll find the proof, based on the federal government's gold standard, experimental research, in the following sources:

Elley, W., & Mangubhai, F. (1983). The impact of reading on second language learning. *Reading Research Quarterly, 19,* 53 – 67.

Elley, W. (1991). Acquiring literacy in a second language: The effect of book-based programs. *Language Learning, 41*(3), 375 – 411.

3. Learning to decode words in context by using the surrounding text can be helpful to students as they learn the alphabetic principle. Shared reading provides this context.

The following quote is from National Reading Panel contributor Steven Stahl in the federally sanctioned book *The Voice of Evidence in Reading Research:*

"Cueing children to use their knowledge of words to decode unknown words in context is an important reading strategy" (p. 191).

Stahl, S. (2004). What do we know about fluency? Findings of the
National Reading Panel. In P. McCardle & V. Chhabra (Eds.),
The voice of evidence in reading research (pp. 187 – 211). Baltimore, MD:
Brookes Publishing.

4. **Students need multiple exposures to new words. Vocabulary is learned more effectively in context than in isolation, and students need opportunities to construct language orally and to use new vocabulary. Shared reading provides that context. In addition, the warm, nonthreatening shared experience invites children to engage actively with and discuss the story. In doing so, new vocabulary is reinforced.**

The quotes below are from National Reading Panel member Michael Kamil in the federally sponsored book *The Voice of Evidence in Reading Research:*

"Not only do students need to encounter vocabulary words frequently, but they should also be given items that are likely to appear in other contexts . . . . The context in which a word is learned is critical. Lists are generally less effective than connected text" (p. 218).

"Structuring vocabulary instruction to include group learning formats has found empirical support . . . . Vocabulary learning should entail active engagement in learning tasks . . . . Students may learn vocabulary . . . . when they are simply listening to other students respond" (p. 219).

Kamil, M. (2004). Vocabulary and comprehension instruction: Summary
and implications of the National Reading Panel findings. In P.
McCardle & V. Chhabra (Eds.), *The voice of evidence in reading research*
(pp. 213 – 234). Baltimore, MD: Brookes Publishing.

5. **Students, especially struggling readers, need support as they are learning to read. They need to experience success and to feel confident they can succeed. Shared reading experiences give students support in reading without the fear of failure.**

The following quote is from Guthrie and Humenick in *The Voice of Evidence in Reading Research:*

"Students with self-efficacy believe they have the capability to read well. They approach books with confidence and tackle challenging texts or difficult words with the expectation that they will master them. They have a 'can do' approach to reading and learning from text. In contrast, students with low self-efficacy are likely to say, 'I can't do it,' when faced with long passages, unfamiliar text, or new expectations for learning from a book. Without the energizing value of high self-efficacy, students are unable to sustain the effort required to learn reading skills or to become knowledgeable through print" (p. 331).

Guthrie, J. T., and Humenick, N. M. (2004). Motivating students to read: Evidence for classroom practices that increase reading motivation and achievement. In P. McCardle & V. Chhabra (Eds.), *The voice of evidence in reading research* (pp. 329 – 354). Baltimore, MD: Brookes Publishing.

A Final Thought

No one method should comprise the entire reading curriculum, and that includes commercial reading programs. We have a wide array of reading methods at our disposal, but research shows that none works all the time for all children.

Just to be clear, *There Was an Old Lady Who Swallowed a Fly* is a delightful book, but like any book or instructional material, it serves some purposes well, and others less so.

Taback, S. (1997). *There was an old lady who swallowed a fly.* New York: Scholastic.

4

Fingerpointing, Voicepointing, and Headpointing

The Tough Question

"I notice that you use your fingers to point while reading. Now my child has picked up this habit. When I was in school, we weren't allowed to use our fingers as a crutch to read. Why are you encouraging this behavior?"

Your Bottom-Line Answer

You Can Say: The federal government's researchers concluded that fingerpoint reading is a necessary stage for children when they're learning to read. I agree with this research, and I encourage fingerpointing early on in the reading process. Here's why:

◆ At first, children don't understand the concept of *speech to print* —that one spoken word equals one written word. This is because we don't clearly separate our words when we talk. We don't pause between words. Instead, we blur the individual words together.

◆ Children need to understand that the spaces in text, the junctures between words, are markers. Early in the process, children often sweep under the text they have previously memorized, with no match at all to the print. They don't track accurately with their eyes or know they are reading individual words. They need to understand the concept of a word as it occurs in written language. Fingerpointing helps them do that.

◆ I can't teach word recognition if my students don't know what a word is. In order for them to understand the alphabetic principle—that speech is made up of sounds that can translate into letters and that those letters make up words that convey meaning in a text—students need to point to the words at first.

◆ Once students have the idea of what words are and can see the similarities and differences among them, your child and I focus on *sweeping through the words in sentences*. Through shared reading of enlarged texts, students learn not just the concept of speech to print, but the importance of fluent, expressive reading.

Fingerpointing is not a bad habit. It's an important developmental stage and instructional tool in reading. I make sure we move past it because it's important for children to know that reading is not about individual letters or even words; it's about meaning. But first I teach what master teacher and author Ardie Cole calls "wordness," within a meaningful text, so children learn this concept without losing sight of our ultimate goal—making sense of all those words we've been pointing to on the page.

Something for You to Think and Talk About

Some children who aren't yet ready to give up the training wheels of fingerpointing engage in what reading researcher Marie Clay calls *voicepointing*. Because they are focusing on speech-to-print word matching, children sound as if they are counting: "1! 2! 3! 4! The! dog! ran! to! the! girl!"

When I read Ardie Cole's description of voicepointing in her book *When Reading Begins*, I laughed out loud:

"Each word is thrust out, like Krispee Kremes popping from the donut machine into the boiling tub of oil below. Their reading may be fast, but each word sounds the same. Identical inflection. Identical pacing. Mechanical. That's voicepointing" (p. 8).

Ardie also notes that beginning readers sometimes keep time with their heads, substituting *headpointing* for fingerpointing. Because they are afraid of losing their place, these readers bob their heads for each word and resemble "those nodding birds that drivers place in car windows" (p. 8), or those bobble-head dolls that have become so popular.

So the big question is: how do you help students move beyond these early word-marking stages? Through shared reading you are already pulling them out of that stage as you model reading fluency. Once students understand wordness, or the concept of speech to print, you can, as Ardie Cole suggests, urge them forward in the process by sliding your finger a little ahead of where you are actually reading.

Pointing to the words isn't as easy as it sounds! Truthfully, I could do it only with relatively short texts with few words per page such as *Mrs. Wishy-Washy* by Joy Cowley. However, there is a real danger in pointing to the words as the children follow along. It's very tempting for teachers to lapse into voicepointing themselves and to punch the words out One! By! One! This is, of course, one of the behaviors in children that we try to overcome by modeling fluency and expression. I've seen this many times with student teachers as they hiccough their way through a big book as the children dutifully voicepoint in response.

If you find yourself doing this, stop and concentrate on your speech-to-print modeling *after* you've all read the story. Remember, word pointing is effective only very early on in the developmental process. We quickly move to more words per page and finger sliding as we read. Think of what you're doing as you read and be careful not to sacrifice fluency to further your goal of teaching "speech to print" by voicepointing to each and every word.

The Proof

You can bolster your argument for the need for early fingerpointing by citing the work of Linnea Ehri, who was a member of the National Reading Panel.

> Ehri, L. C, & Sweet, J. S. (1991). Fingerpoint reading of memorized text: What enables beginners to process the print? *Reading Research Quarterly, 26*, 442 – 62.

To gain a deeper understanding of the evolution of early reading behaviors, see the following books:

> Clay, M. M. (1979). *Reading: The patterning of complex behavior.* Portsmouth, NH: Heinemann.

> Cole, A. D. (2004). *When reading begins: The teacher's role in decoding, comprehension and fluency.* Portsmouth, NH: Heinemann.

A Final Thought

When we focus on isolated skills instruction, we give children the message that reading is about skills and saying words. Even once they move past the physical act of fingerpointing, if children's minds are still focused on individual letters and words instead of the meaning of the text as a whole, they will be just as hobbled as if they were using the crutch of pointing with their fingers. Think about it.

5

Worksheets and Homework

The Tough Question

" *My son used to bring home worksheets he completed in school and worksheets for homework, too. When I was in school we did workbooks all the time to learn reading. Why don't you send worksheets home with my son?* "

Your Bottom-Line Answer

You Can Say: I'm going to answer your question about worksheets and then I'll discuss the issue of homework. I know that teachers assign worksheets as homework with the very best of intentions. Many teachers believe that they keep kids off the streets and away from the television. However, there is no research to support using worksheets at school or at home. Experimental research shows that the way we learn skills affects how we use them. In other words, skills taught and practiced out of the context of real reading often do not transfer into reading and comprehending connected text. Students think the skills are just for the worksheets or, even more troubling, that reading is about skills instead of meaning. There are many other reasons why worksheets don't teach skills appropriately:

- Students quickly pick up the pattern of the worksheets and can complete them without really even understanding what they're doing.

- Most worksheets are part of commercial programs and follow a set sequence of skills rather than addressing the unique academic needs of students. I know this from my own observations, but federal researchers confirm it.

- Often worksheets focus on only one or two skills at a time. Real reading doesn't work that way.

- In order to complete the worksheets—on a vowel sound like short *a*, for example—students already have to know the skill. Therefore, worksheets don't really teach. They are a form of assessment, not instruction.

- Worksheets aren't good for practicing skills, either, because they don't involve application of skills in the real reading (or writing) of connected text. Research shows that skills should be taught simultaneously with context.

- If we are brutally honest about it, worksheets are boring. Research shows students must be actively engaged and motivated to learn.

- Worksheets and workbooks are extremely expensive. They are termed "consumables" because they get used up and we have to keep purchasing them. Since research shows they are not just boring but ineffective, I don't want to waste the taxpayers' money by buying them.

Worksheets and other mindless "busywork" ease the workload of teachers. We can just move through the packets without planning or thinking. But they are a waste of instructional time, and so I don't use them.

As for assigning worksheets as homework, I also feel that it is an intrusion into your at-home time with your child. Students have a long day in school, and when they get home, like you, they deserve family time, not more skill and drill. There is no research that proves homework has any positive effect on grades or student performance. Wasteful busywork and grueling amounts of homework are not respectful of your family time. I use our class time intelligently and efficiently. I have no business intruding into your home life when research shows it doesn't help anyway.

Something for You to Think and Talk About

I want to share something that I've observed through my years in education and that I hope you'll think about and maybe discuss with your colleagues. I believe that when children first come to school, they hate worksheets and resist completing them. However, after having them assigned day after day, week after week, and month after month, a sad transformation takes place. I believe students grow comfortable with worksheets not because they help them learn, but because they are mindless. Kids can just tune out and complete them without thought.

When you look at the format of worksheets honestly, you see prescribed little spaces for prescribed little answers. And so, students aren't just figuratively forced to "think inside the box"; students must *literally stay* within the boxes, the little boxes on the page. Little spaces, little thinking. After weeks and months of conditioned responses to prescribed worksheet formats, conformity becomes comfortable. And real thinking—the construction of original thought articulated in real language—becomes a threat.

I really don't believe that the blank stares and the tuned-out expressions of so many students are simply a consequence of changing attitudes as they grow older. I believe this because I've seen classrooms in which intermediate and high school students are excited and energetic, vibrant and involved in learning. We need to consider that maybe the school curriculum has trained many students into that passivity. I hope you'll think about that and see if you've noticed that transformation, too.

Worksheets and workbooks are usually part of commercial reading programs. Government-sponsored research and researchers caution against using them.

The Proof

1. "Normal instruction" in school curricula often involves teachers assigning worksheets from commercial programs. This is counterproductive.

The following quote is by Timothy Shanahan, who is on President Bush's Literacy Panel, was a member of the National Reading Panel, and is a federally approved government researcher:

"What is 'normal instruction'? It often turned out that the kids were assigned random worksheets. What a terrible definition of teaching! Assigning random worksheets is just dopey" (p. 14).

> Shanahan, T. (2006, June – July). President's message: Does he really think kids shouldn't read? *Reading Today.*

2. Commercial reading programs and their materials follow a set sequence and do not meet the unique needs of all students.

Here you can again cite the phonics section of *The Report of the National Reading Panel,* the federal government's gold standard for reading research:

"At all grade levels but particularly in kindergarten and the early grades it is common for children to vary greatly in the skills they bring to school" (Summary Booklet, p. 11).

"It is common for many phonics programs to present a fixed sequence of lessons scheduled from the beginning to the end of the school year" (p. 2-97).

> National Institute of Child Health and Human Development. (2000). *The report of the National Reading Panel: Report of the subgroups (phonics) and summary booklet.* Washington, DC: U.S. Government Printing Office. The report can be accessed and obtained free at www.nationalreadingpanel.org

Note: The NRP did not recommend that teachers use commercial reading programs. In fact, it warned against their use and consistently confirmed that teachers need to be decision makers and individualize, rather than standardize, instruction.

3. There is no research that shows homework helps.

This quote is from Alfie Kohn's book *The Homework Myth: Why Our Kids Get Too Much of a Bad Thing*:

"Most of us are familiar with the disadvantages of homework: stress, family conflict, lost time for other activities, and diminution of interest in learning. What's surprising is that there are actually few, if any, pros to off-set these cons. A review of the latest research (1) finds that homework provides absolutely no academic benefits for younger students, (2) raises serious questions about such benefits for older students, and (3) fails to support the belief that homework promotes independence, responsibility, or good work habits. The interesting question, then, is why we continue to assign, or accept, homework in the absence of supporting data" (p. 74).

> Kohn, A. (2006). *The homework myth: Why our kids get too much of a bad thing.* Cambridge, MA: Da Capo Press.

4. Students need to be actively engaged, rather than passive and bored, or they don't learn. Worksheets require routine responses and encourage passivity rather than excitement about learning.

The following is a statement by former assistant secretary of education Susan Neuman. It was released at the White House Summit on Early Childhood Cognitive Development:

"For too many of our children, instruction fails to 'engage their minds.' Children's minds atrophy with limited stimuli."

> Neuman, S. (2001, July 27). Access to print: Problem, consequences and day-one solutions. Press release on early childhood cognitive development. Washington, DC: Department of Education.

A Final Thought

Like me, perhaps you can think back to your experiences with worksheets in school. I remember mindlessly grinding my way through them and being so bored I could almost scream. When you think back to completing worksheets when you were in school, do you recall being actively engaged with them? Did they excite and challenge you and truly make you think? And I'd ask you to honestly recall how you felt about homework. Do you believe that for the most part it really extended your learning? Did you care about what you were doing? Or did you just get through it as fast as you could?

As a matter of fact, many parents are now rebelling against the amount and type of homework that intrudes into their home life. If what we do is to be research based, then we need to face the reality that research simply does not support the use of homework.

6

Commercial Reading Programs and Guided Reading

The Tough Question

When I was in school, my teachers used series of reading books for reading instruction. They had all kinds of stories in them all under one cover. Instead, you use individual books for reading groups. Why don't you use those reading series that I was taught to read from and other teachers in the school use for instruction?

Your Bottom-Line Answer

You Can Say: Those commercial reading series you asked about are also called *basal readers*. When I first started teaching, I relied on them very heavily for structure and guidance. I still refer to them for ideas. However, I have learned a lot since then. The federal government's research does not support the use of commercial reading series, and through experience I've come to recognize their limitations as well:

- ◆ Research shows that commercial reading programs are less effective than programs that rely on "real" reading material. In fact, reading test scores from states that select and mandate commercial texts are lower than so-called "free territories" that don't require texts.

- ◆ Often, the stories in basals are all in one leveled book or *anthology*. This is not the way we read in the real world. We don't pick up a single book with fiction and nonfiction all under one cover. This may seem trivial, but it isn't. My job is to prepare students to use literacy in real life. So I need to make our in-school reading resemble real reading as much as possible.

- ◆ Research shows that commercial reading programs flit from topic to topic rather than encouraging in-depth study of topics. Often the activities listed in the teacher's manual do not follow a logical sequence or have logical connections to the activities in other sections. Sometimes they don't even relate directly to the stories the students read.

- ◆ Because basal readers have many stories crammed under a single cover, the stories are often shortened. In other words, they are *abridged*. Sadly, when stories are abridged, they lose their flavor and a lot of the rich language and nuances that made them great in the first place!

- ◆ Sometimes the reading materials in the basals are not even abridged stories with a beginning, a middle, and an end. Instead, they are *excerpts*, a few pages cut out of some section of a book. These fragments of stories are harmful to comprehension. They don't make sense. I've noticed that those excerpts teach my students that written language does not have a formal structure. Eventually, students just tune out because they no longer expect written material to be satisfying. The idea behind having students read excerpts is that students will be hooked by the fragment of the story and will then get the book and read it. At first I believed in this concept, but then I discovered it really doesn't happen.

For one thing, our library doesn't have enough copies of the same book for all our students. I don't have enough money in my classroom budget to buy enough books, either. So I soon figured out that instead of wasting your money on pieces of books in expensive series, it is smarter and more economical to buy the original books from our book club flyers in the first place.

- Those basal readers are not sold alone. Schools purchase accompanying materials such as workbooks and worksheets. These are called *consumables* because they get used up and need to be repurchased. These commercial reading series are not free. They are extremely expensive. I save taxpayers a lot of money by using research-proven alternatives. I would rather use the money to purchase real books such as those in the book club flyers that I send home with your child. Those books can be used again and again and I teach many reading skills through real stories.

- Sometimes the stories in basals are written not for the sake of the story but for word practice: few words are introduced before reading, and the so-called "stories" are written for practice of the target words in context. Again, over time I noticed that these nonstories for word practice are boring. The language is stilted and unnatural. I want your child to love reading. What's more, those nonstories are as bad as excerpts in that they give students the idea that reading isn't supposed to make sense. They are harmful to comprehension.

- My teaching focuses far more on comprehension and higher-level thinking than do basal consumables, which stress low-level comprehension questions. I do this through lots of group discussion and thinking about real text. I want your child to be a thinker, a leader, and not a follower.

- Another drawback of commercial reading series are the teacher's *manuals* that come along with them. Research shows that the manuals often require teachers to follow a strict sequence of activities and even to read from a script. This standardizes instruction. But it also standardizes your child. You know and I know that your child is unique. She is not a widget on an assembly line. Teaching by simply following a manual is easy for teachers. We don't have to plan or think very much. But many of my colleagues and I believe that the extra work involved in applying the research and teaching reading skills in context and according to students' unique skills is worth the extra time and effort.

Commercial reading programs can be useful tools, especially for beginning teachers. But in time, most of us recognize and come to agree with the scientific research on reading: no one program and no one method should constitute the entire reading curriculum. In time, we learn to grow beyond them. After all, those programs were written by people who have never been in my classroom and who don't know your child the way I do. So instead of using expensive, ineffective reading series that standardize instruction, I do what the research recommends: I individualize instruction, and I teach reading skills through a balanced approach using many methods, including assisted guided reading.

What follows is a description of the steps in assisted guided reading. This can help you to articulate the process to parents, administrators, and teachers in professional development workshops.

- First, I place students in small groups (no more than six) based on instructional reading level, which I determine through individual, ongoing assessment (running records). This is the level that is just a little challenging but not frustrating—the level at which your child can read with 90 to 95 percent accuracy. In assisted guided reading, each student has his or her own book, encouraging a bit more independence and offering more challenge than shared reading or read-alouds.

- Second, I do what's called a *book walk*. As a group, we talk about what the story will be about and how it connects to the students' own lives. For example, if it's a story about losing a tooth, I get the students to talk about their experiences losing teeth (a big deal for first graders!). I do something very smart and research-proven at this point. I have the students go through the book with me and put their fingers on hard words and vocabulary that might challenge them as they read on their own. Sometimes, I have the students write the new words on whiteboards or create them with magnetic letters. I also do this direct, phonics-vocabulary instruction *after* we've read the story. My goal is to provide lots of exposures to new words and opportunities to practice spelling and phonics skills in a way that makes sense!

  I used to put new words on the board and go through them with my students before we started reading. But since I've studied the federal government's research on vocabulary instruction, I have found that I can teach vocabulary using *direct instruction*—by having children find and discuss new vocabulary in context—before and after reading. This approach is far more effective than teaching words in isolation! It gives students a hook. They can hang those new words on something meaningful, and my teaching is much more likely to stick.

- Third, after the children and I have skimmed through every page of the story and pointed to new words and vocabulary, they read the story to themselves in a soft voice while I move around with my clipboard taking notes as I listen to and assist the children. At this time I also do informal assessment of individual needs, including taking *running records*. I write down exactly what your child reads so I can analyze the errors, or miscues. I see what skills your child needs to learn and then I work specifically on those skills. The federal government's *Report of the National Reading Panel* warns against a rigid curriculum that doesn't account for individual differences. That research made sense to me and has influenced how I teach. I treat your child as an individual who is unique instead of using one-size-fits-all instruction.

- Fourth, after the children have read the story, I use follow-up activities, including drawing and writing responses to the story—maybe letters to the characters or "book reviews" for their classmates to read—and I engage my class in lots of discussion about stories, too. In this way, your child is using the new vocabulary and extending what she learned in the story. To learn new vocabulary, students need to use the words, and that means letting them talk and construct language instead of just repeating it. That just makes sense, doesn't it?

I've quit using worksheets for skills and vocabulary practice because they don't actively engage children and are boring. Research recommends active teacher involvement on a personal level with students. Therefore, my goal is to help your child maintain a personal connection to the story and to help her expand on and practice the skills she has learned in a way that is meaningful and keeps her engaged!

Something for You to Think and Talk About

A lot of the explanations for the research-based methods of assisted guided reading focus on what is good for the children, and of course that should be our primary concern. However, our level of involvement, enthusiasm, and professionalism as teachers is also important. We matter, too. We should not be separated from the teaching-learning process. A student's teacher should be a thoughtful, flesh-and-blood person—not a commercial manual. That is central to the federal government's research. *The Report of the National Reading Panel* states that some commercial reading programs "are scripted in such a way that teacher judgment is largely eliminated. Although scripts may standardize instruction, they may reduce teachers' interest in the teaching process" (p. 2-96).

The report also says, "It seems evident that teachers will be most effective when they are enthusiastic in their teaching and enjoy what they are doing in their classrooms" (p. 2-7).

Commercial reading programs can offer lots of good ideas, especially for new teachers, and can provide a useful structure and a guide for the skills, including phonics sounds, that we need to teach. However, there's a temptation at times to adhere strictly to a commercial reading program or even follow scripted lessons. Doing so takes less time than planning lessons from scratch, and that can feel like a definite advantage. But what do we sacrifice when a commercial program defines the entire reading curriculum?

Shifting into teacher's-manual cruise control and reciting from the script by rote comes with a big price tag, literally and figuratively. I'm suggesting that you consider your own role in the teaching-learning process. How much are you willing to standardize your instruction and, in the process, become standardized yourself?

The Proof

1. **Research shows that in "textbook adoption states" students score lower in reading and other subjects than those in "free territory" states. Commercial texts limit and dumb down the curriculum by teaching to the lowest common denominator. The text is sanitized and abridged and flits from topic to topic, thus interfering with comprehension and higher-level thinking skills.**

The following quote is from a study reported by nationally recognized education critic Diane Ravitch and Chester Finn, who served as the assistant secretary for research and improvement at the U.S. Department of Education:

"The painful truth is that today's textbooks fail students—and are directly implicated in the poor showing that U.S. youngsters make in international achievement tests . . . . A 2002 survey of elementary and high school teachers found that about 80 percent use textbooks in their classrooms . . . . They were so dumbed down, and flitted so relentlessly from topic to topic, that American schoolchildren were learning less than their peers."

Finn, C., & Ravitch, D. (2004). *The mad, mad world of textbook adoption*. Available from the Fordham Foundation: www.edexcellence.net/institute/publication/publication.cfm?id=335

2. **Commercial texts leech subject matter of interest and relevance by dumbing down the rich language and context that make literature, history, and other subjects meaningful to students. The same problem is common with commercial basal series, since the stories they include are often abridged or written for word practice.**

The following quote is also from Diane Ravitch and Chester Finn:

"It takes little imagination to see that student ignorance and disinterest are nurtured by boilerplate writing and chock-a-block, narrative-deprived textbooks. Not surprisingly, these glorified encyclopedias make poor nighttime-reading companions . . . . Invariably, today's textbooks are described as deadly bores, incapable of telling a story or providing a compelling narrative, and lacking any author's voice.

"Instead, students struggle through coffee-table-style textbooks, weighed down with graphics, editorial cartoons, sidebars, color illustrations, boxes, and goofy exercises. These door-stoppers—which average 750 to 1,100 pages in length—are so heavy that the Consumer Product Safety Commission has warned that an 'overweight backpack' phenomenon may be sending thousands of children to emergency rooms with back and neck injuries . . . .

"Every reviewer of American textbooks reports that they consist of politically blanched, dumbed-down text, larded with disconnected facts that are sometimes erroneous and not infrequently misleading."

Finn, C., & Ravitch, D. (2004). *The mad, mad world of textbook adoption.* Available from the Fordham Foundation: www.edexcellence.net/institute/publication/publication.cfm?id=335

3. **Federal research recommends assisted guided reading, including personalized teacher monitoring and responses to student reading behaviors, as opposed to the standardized exercises in text-driven curricula. The federal research also cites Marie Clay's work on the importance of helping students use context to decode and cross-check the meanings of unknown words.**

This next quote is from National Reading Panel contributor Steven Stahl in the federally sanctioned book *The Voice of Evidence in Reading Research*:

"Reading instruction is most effective when teachers actively monitor students as they are reading by 'cueing children to use their knowledge of words to decode unknown words in context' (Clay, 1993) and assisting them in recognizing and correcting miscues" (p. 209).

> Stahl, S. (2004). What do we know about fluency? Findings of the National Reading Panel. In P. McCardle & V. Chhabra (Eds.), *The voice of evidence in reading research* (pp. 187 – 211). Baltimore, MD: Brookes Publishing.

4. The National Reading Panel cautions against the use of commercial reading series and standardized skills instruction, and emphasizes the importance of active teacher engagement and decision making in the instructional process.

You'll find this next quote in *The Report of the National Reading Panel: Report of the Subgroups (Phonics)*:

"The lack of attention to motivational factors by researchers in the design of phonics programs [as part of a basal reading series] is potentially very serious because debates about reading instruction often boil down to concern about the 'relevance' and 'interest value' of how something is being taught, rather than specific content of what is being taught" (p. 2-97).

> National Institute of Child Health and Human Development. (2000). *The report of the National Reading Panel: Report of the subgroups (phonics)*. Washington, DC: U.S. Government Printing Office. The report can be accessed and obtained free at www.nationalreadingpanel.org

5. Nowhere in the NRP report do the federal government's researchers recommend that commercial programs should be used to teach reading, nor do they recommend any specific reading program. In fact, the report's findings as well as its direct recommendations caution against the use of commercial phonics programs.

The following is a quote from Timothy Shanahan on the video entitled *Teaching Children to Read, 2nd edition*, distributed by the National Reading

Panel. Shanahan was a member of the NRP and was appointed to George W. Bush's federal Literacy Panel. The video is available for free at www. nationalreadingpanel.org. Click Documents to order.

"The schools are barraged with commercial products and gurus who come through with some new product or magic cure for children's reading needs. We must stop looking for 'the magic bullet' because there is none."

6. Assisted guided reading provides opportunities for students to read connected text as well as to use new vocabulary in group discussions of "real" stories in "real" books as opposed to contrived stories in basal readers.

This next quote is by federally sanctioned researcher Michael Kamil in *The Voice of Evidence in Reading Research*:

"Structuring vocabulary instruction to include group learning formats has found empirical support . . . . Vocabulary learning should entail active engagement in learning tasks . . . . Students may learn vocabulary . . . . when they are simply listening to other students respond."

Kamil, M. (2004). Vocabulary and comprehension instruction: Summary and implications of the National Reading Panel findings. In P. McCardle & V. Chhabra (Eds.), *The voice of evidence in reading research* (pp. 213 – 234). Baltimore, MD: Brookes Publishing.

7

Independent Reading or Sustained Silent Reading (SSR)

The Tough Question

"Why do you allow students to read on their own during class? When they are reading silently to themselves, how do you know they're really reading? Shouldn't you be testing them and making sure they're reading the right level of book? It seems to me there are a lot of problems with just having the class read on its own."

Your Bottom-Line Answer

You Can Say: Research overwhelmingly shows that the more time students spend reading, the better they get at it—just like practice in music and sports. What's more, the benefits of sustained silent reading (SSR) have far-reaching effects. Good readers do better in other subjects as well because as students learn to read, they are also *reading to learn.*

However, research also shows me how to use SSR most effectively in my classroom. When I'm implementing SSR with my students, I vary my own degree of engagement with them according to their individual needs. I also tend to let students read more on their own, without my involvement, as the year goes on and they've grown in independence and ability. I take steps to make sure students choose books at the right level and are truly engaged in reading instead of being off task. Here's what I do to make sure they are not "goofing off":

- ◆ I let students choose their own books from a selection of high-interest books I keep in the classroom. The scientific research of Warwick Elley shows that a good selection of high-interest books in classrooms is a big step in encouraging students to read and improving their reading ability.

- ◆ Some students may at times choose a book that's not at their reading level. I don't worry too much if a book is too easy, because easy books serve a purpose, too. They help with fluency and build confidence, especially for struggling readers. To help students avoid books that are too hard, I do "book sells" in small groups, targeting the appropriate reading level for the students in that group. I talk about a selection of books and generate students' curiosity. This is similar to what we as adults do when we are excited about a book. We "sell" it to our friends.

- ◆ After they have read, I encourage student discussion. I talk to students about the book they're reading, what they liked and what they didn't. I do this casually, as adults do in book clubs. I do not lapse into "testing mode." I want reading to be fun, not a punishment.

- ◆ I keep a variety of reading materials in the room, not just books. I have a selection of magazines, poetry, nonfiction, and even certain comic books. Students, especially boys, often love silly, even outlandish books such as the Captain Underpants series by Dav Pilkey. Girls really love the Junie B. Jones series by Barbara Park.

- I find that many students respond to books by imitating the writing of their favorite authors. Many boys like to make their own versions of Captain Underpants complete with illustrations. They love comic books, too, and they often write their own. I encourage them to do this as a response to books. These student-authored books can then become part of our class library.

- My classroom library also has many picture books. Yes, they tend to have fewer words than more sophisticated books, but they are also attractive to students, and the pictures can help struggling readers and English language learners to understand the text.

- I want to send my students the right message. They learn what I value not by what I say but by what I do. If I believe that reading is important, then I need to find time for it and trust students to read in school. What's more, they need to see me reading, too. I do not grade papers or chat in the hallway with the teacher in the next room while my students are reading. I read my own book, showing them that I respect the process.

- SSR is not my complete reading program. It is the culmination of all the assisted reading methods I use, including read-alouds, shared reading, guided reading, and direct skills instruction.

The goal of any reading instruction is to help students become literate so they can function in society when they're out of school. We don't go through life with someone helping us read. If I didn't allow students to experience independent reading—our ultimate goal—right here in my classroom, I wouldn't be doing my job.

Something for You to Think and Talk About

One of the criticisms of SSR is that we can't tell if students are really reading or if they're daydreaming or "goofing off" in some other nonacademic way. I find this argument intriguing.

It's true enough that when students are reading silently we can't control what is going on inside their heads. But on the other hand, when can we control what students are thinking or what they are learning? When we talk, how can we know they are really listening? They may be sitting quietly in their seats, but how do we know their minds aren't a million miles away? How do we know that students who complete worksheets or other seatwork really care about the assignments and aren't just going through the motions to get their grade?

If we allow students time to read in class, it's true, we *don't* know if they're concentrating, much less comprehending, and it is a temptation to try to control the learning by asking comprehension questions. But if we do that, what have we accomplished? If our purpose is to help students experience the joys of reading, then does testing them afterward really help to achieve that goal, or is it more likely to turn the act of reading into a stressful chore? What does it say about our beliefs about reading if students know we don't trust them to really read when we give them a chance to do so?

I think we've all experienced daydreaming or faking our way through classes and assignments. I recall "reading" pages of textbooks and then realizing I couldn't recall a word I'd read. The hard truth is that we can control the classroom environment and external factors. To an extent, at least, we can exert some control over and manage student behavior. But we can't control students' attitudes, and we cannot control whether or not they choose to learn. So, the best we can do is make material inviting, actively involve students in the learning process, and practice what we preach. "Literacy is important," we should say. "Reading is fun. That's why I trust you to read when I give you time to do so."

I think that for teachers, giving up control to students is not just difficult—it's terrifying. It feels like a free fall. Nevertheless, at some point, if the purpose of schooling is to prepare students for life in society, we must allow them to assume responsibility for their own learning. At some point, we need to take that leap of faith, free fall, and allow students to assume control of their own learning. If we believe what we say about the intrinsic value of reading, then don't we need to show instead of tell—and let students read?

I want to recommend a book by Nancie Atwell here, *The Reading Zone*. This short, easy-to-read book took my breath away. It's not only a passionate appeal for allowing kids to read in school, it is the result of her own action research. The book is not just a theoretical argument. It offers a variety of methods for implementing and organizing a literate classroom. Warning: It is also provocative. There are parts of it that may even anger you, but it will definitely make you think and provoke conversation.

Atwell, N. (2006). *The reading zone: How to help kids become skilled, passionate, habitual, critical readers.* New York: Scholastic.

The Proof

Sustained silent reading with high-interest books increases not only vocabulary and reading ability but writing proficiency as well.

The quote below is from the summary booklet of *The Report of the National Reading Panel*:

"There is widespread agreement in the literature that encouraging students to engage in wide, independent, silent reading increases reading achievement. Literally hundreds of correlational studies find that the best readers read the most and that poor readers read the least. These correlational studies suggest that the more children read, the better their reading vocabulary and comprehension" (p. 12).

> National Institute of Child Health and Human Development. (2000). *The report of the National Reading Panel: Summary booklet*. Washington, DC: U.S. Government Printing Office. The report can be accessed and obtained free at www.nationalreadingpanel.org

These next quotes are from NRP contributor and researcher Steven Stahl. Both are from the federally sanctioned book *The Voice of Evidence in Reading Research*:

"Teachers should arrange for students to choose their own books or other reading materials for at least 30 minutes of independent reading every day with books of the students' own choice" (p. 201).

"The more time students spend 'with eyes on text,' or doing engaged reading, the better readers they become" (p. 190).

> Stahl, S. (2004). What do we know about fluency? Findings of the National Reading Panel. In P. McCardle & V. Chhabra (Eds.), *The voice of evidence in reading research* (pp. 187 – 211). Baltimore, MD: Brookes Publishing.

Stahl's quote of the phrase "eyes on text" is from the following source:

> Berliner, D. C. (1981). Academic learning time and reading achievement. In J. T. Guthrie (Ed.), *Comprehension and teaching: Research reviews* (pp. 203 – 226). Newark, DE: International Reading Association.

One more important federally approved research document you need to be aware of is *What Research Reveals*. It was written by Susan Neuman, a former assistant secretary of education. The purpose of this government document was to help teachers implement scientific research in response to No Child Left Behind. This research document is very easy to read and is packed with wonderful information and good quotes for workshops and newsletters. Here is a quote from it:

"[Teachers should] schedule independent reading and writing periods in literacy-rich classrooms [to] provide children with opportunities to select books of their own choosing. They may engage in the social activities of reading with their peers, asking questions and writing stories."

Neuman, S. B. (2001, November). *What research reveals: Foundations of reading instruction in preschool and primary education.* Washington, DC: United States Department of Education. I highly recommend that you get it online, at www.rmcres.com/documents/what_research_reveals.pdf

To Literacy Coaches, Workshop Providers, and Administrators

If you're preparing for a workshop, I hope you'll take special note of the "book flood" studies and describe them to your audience.

Warwick Elley (the same researcher who did the study on the effects of read-alouds on vocabulary acquisition cited in Question 1) and Francis Mangubhai did a series of longitudinal studies in dozens of schools with thousands of children ranging in age from 6 to 12. These landmark studies are known as the "book flood" studies. There are several factors that make the studies particularly relevant to teachers:

1. As with Elley's vocabulary study on the impact of read-alouds on children's vocabulary, the studies used an experimental "medical model" and therefore meet the government's rigorous criteria—the gold standard for research.

2. These studies examined the effects of SSR and shared reading on children whose first language was not English but who were required to learn English. Thus, the findings have astounding applications for teachers who have English language learners in their classrooms.

3. The control groups in the studies—the children who did not engage in SSR or shared reading—were in classrooms in which the teacher used a formal English/grammar/reading program structured around what Elley calls a "neat, set series of lessons." Thus, the materials in the control group resemble the commercial reading programs used in many classrooms. Teachers introduce new vocabulary words out of context, in isolation. They teach formal grammar skills also in isolation. Children then practice those skills on worksheets and finally read stories with limited, controlled vocabulary.

4. The studies involved a wide range of grade levels, from first grade to intermediate school.

The Methods of the Book Flood Studies

The methods and materials are important for us to understand. The schools in the study were "flooded" with a large number of high-interest books. There were actually three different methods that were researched: shared reading, SSR, and a commercial program. Teachers in the two experimental groups were provided with a day of professional development training in providing shared assisted reading. They were shown how to engage children in shared reading using lots of discussion, interactions, drawing, and acting out of stories to familiarize them with vocabulary before reading, activities such as those I described earlier in this book.

The SSR group of teachers were a less active group. They did read to the students and they displayed books and talked about them, but the majority of the interactions with books were in the form of SSR. The students in that group read for at least 30 minutes a day.

The Results of the Book Flood Studies

The results of the series of book flood studies were compelling. Students in both the shared reading and SSR groups significantly outperformed those in the formally structured commercial program (the control group) in reading comprehension, vocabulary, and writing skills. In other words, just providing high-interest books and allowing students time to read proved to be more successful than using structured, sequenced lessons from a commercial reading series. Think about that.

The shared reading group outperformed the SSR group, but again, both groups made significant progress. In fact, the increase in writing skills actually came as a surprise to the researchers because writing was not part of the instruction. What this suggests is that there is a strong link between reading and writing. You can cite and I hope even read the following for information on the book flood studies:

Elley, W., & Mangubhai, F. (1983). The impact of reading on second language learning. *Reading Research Quarterly, 19,* 53 – 67.

Elley, W. (1991). Acquiring literacy in a second language: The effect of book-based programs. *Language Learning, 41*(3), 375 – 411.

Reading

8

Rewards and the Accelerated Reader Program

The Tough Question

In other classes, the teachers give rewards like stickers and parties for kids who read a lot. You don't do that. Why is my child missing out on the inspiration of rewards for reading and completing her work?

Your Bottom-Line Answer

You Can Say: My teaching is based on scientific, evidence-based research. There is no scientific, much less federally approved, research to support the use of the Accelerated Reader program (AR). In fact, the little research that does exist shows AR doesn't help. Therefore, I do not use it. The reward for reading is reading itself. If I hand out stickers and points for reading books, I give students the message that reading is such an unpleasant chore that I have to bribe them to do it. Research supports the need to encourage students' internal, personal motivation for reading and learning rather than their dependence on external rewards. There are other problems with giving points and rewards for the number of books read:

◆ I don't want to give students the idea that reading is about quantity instead of quality so they rush through books to get their points. Books should be savored.

◆ I've noticed, and research has shown, that as soon as the rewards or points are removed, students stop reading. The act of reading becomes tightly linked to external incentives instead of the pleasure of reading.

◆ Programs that give children points for books limit students. Research shows that students don't read books that are not on the programs' accepted book lists. This proves that the motivation for reading is the points—and not the love of reading.

◆ The computerized tests that students must take after reading a book use low-level questions that focus on trivial details. This trains students to think little and low instead of high and deep. I want your child to be a thinker and doer—a leader.

◆ My goal is to help your child become a lifelong reader and learner. Sending him the message that there's no point to reading or learning without some sort of external perk doesn't help to achieve that goal.

Something for You to Think and Talk About

The argument *for* giving external rewards for reading is that, yes, first students will be attracted by the rewards, but eventually they will be hooked by the books and the rewards won't matter anymore. What I hope you'll think about is that sometimes we teach lessons we don't intend to teach at all.

Our actions send messages to students about what we value, and sometimes those subtle, unspoken messages speak more loudly than our words. It's always bothered me that for all the shouting about the joys of reading and for all the posters hung around schools celebrating reading, some teachers still think they need to bribe students to read.

Another problem with giving rewards that's even more troublesome is that children don't come to us with equal abilities and opportunities. The playing field isn't level. Therefore, rewards can become punishments or humiliations for some students. When I was a reading specialist, I recall going into a kindergarten classroom. The teacher had charts for various skills posted on the wall. One listed the names of the children who learned their colors, another listed the names of those who knew shapes, and yet another listed the students' names and displayed stars for the sight words they'd learned. There, posted for all to see, were the names of the little kindergartners who had no stars next to their names or just one or two stars, in stark contrast to the high achievers with multiple stars. Those charts and the others I've seen displayed in classrooms over the years have haunted me. I wonder what long-term damage is done to children when we publicly display their failures.

What I found particularly puzzling is that the teacher was a close friend of mine and, in most ways, one of the kindest, most empathetic people I've ever known. Somehow, though, she just didn't make the connection that she was embarrassing and marginalizing the less able children, or understand that perhaps some of those kids were just a little behind developmentally and that she was punishing them for something over which they had little or no control. I learned a lesson early on in my teaching career. When I was working with students, I gave out lots of stickers, but I never attached them to performance. I just said, "I liked these stickers and I thought you would, too." It's something to think about.

Accelerated Reader

The truth is, there is no federally sponsored or independent research that I know of that supports the Accelerated Reader program. There is, however, research on external versus internal motivation that I'll cite in "The Proof" section for this question. Some of the research on AR is suspect because it's sponsored by the company itself and is posted on its Web site rather than being done by objective researchers and published in peer-reviewed journals. And the fact that there is no scientific research to support its use is reason enough not to use it. Don't forget, our teaching needs to be justified by scientific research.

As for programs like AR that award points when kids read if they can pass a computerized reading test, we need to question the effects of that practice. I myself believe that AR *does* get kids excited about the prospect of earning points. I also believe that it does get kids "reading." But if by *reading* we mean having an active engagement with books that becomes part of a lifelong disposition to read, then AR raises a lot of serious questions.

The computerized tests the students take focus on low-level comprehension questions—trivial details—instead of important ideas and critical thinking. If students read one or two or even three books and answer low-level questions afterward, it might not do much good, but there's no real harm done. But if answering those low-level questions becomes a routine—a consistent, ongoing, and integral part of students' reading lives—then there are unintended and negative consequences: students may come to believe that the purpose of reading is not just to acquire points but to focus on unimportant details in a story so they can answer questions on the computer. Thus, they will be trained to read superficially. One teacher confided to me that she believes that over time AR actually trains students to "think dumb."

Furthermore, you don't need to rely solely on outside research, since in the case of AR there is little objective data. You can be a researcher in your own classroom. Keep the ideas I've suggested in this section in mind and observe your students. If you give rewards for learning or points for AR, consider what values you are transmitting about reading. Should reading invite students to be part of a literate community engaged in literate discourse, or is it enough to make it a solitary act, the goal of which is answering questions to score points? Are rewards a quick fix that actually do long-term damage to students' beliefs about reading and learning? Listen to what your students say when they talk among themselves. Are they eagerly discussing the wonderful books they've read and why they loved them—or are they comparing who has the most points? If you'd like to conduct an experiment to see if rewards lead to a love of literature, remove the rewards and see what happens.

Then, observe and interpret the implications of your evidence as a whole. Weigh that evidence. Determine if the external rewards eclipse the intrinsic value of reading and learning. What evidence do you have that students ever move beyond those incentives to love reading and to become lifelong learners? That's the big question.

There is overwhelming, very powerful research to support the idea that reading aloud to students and engaging them in independent reading has an enormous influence on their reading ability. That being the case, does it make sense to muddy the clarity of that process with bribes?

The Proof

1. *"Despite the popularity of AR, we must conclude that there is no real evidence supporting it, no evidence that the additional tests and rewards add anything to the power of simply supplying access to high-quality and interesting reading material and providing time for children to read them"* (p. 24).

> Krashen, S. D. (2002). Accelerated Reader: Does it work? If so, why? *School Libraries in Canada, 22*(2), 24 – 27.

It's also worth checking out and citing Stephen Krashen's other research on Accelerated Reader, as well as his many articles about the power of reading. Check his Web site, www.sdkrashen.com, for a fair and balanced overview of the research (or lack thereof) on Accelerated Reader. Also, see the following article:

> Krashen, S. D. (2003). The (lack of) experimental evidence supporting the use of Accelerated Reader. *Journal of Children's Literature, 29*(2), 16 – 30.

2. *The Report of the National Reading Panel* **notes the lack of scientific research on AR.**

"*The studies that do exist are of questionable quality and they do not show that AR is more effective than other methods. The NRP does not recommend the use of AR*" (p. 3-26).

> National Institute of Child Health and Human Development. (2000). *The report of the National Reading Panel: Report of the subgroups (fluency).* Washington, DC: U.S. Government Printing Office.

3. Accelerated Reader raises many questions about the long-term damage it may do to students' higher-level thinking skills and attitudes about reading.

The following quotes are from Linda Labbo, who did a comprehensive research study on Accelerated Reader:

"For all practical purposes, the AR quizzes that appear on the computer screen are electronic versions of the questions that used to be listed at the end of reading passages or on worksheets in basal reading series of the past. The psychometric properties of the instrument make it more like a standardized testing situation than a rich forum for reflecting on text. Shouldn't we be raising questions about basalizing and standardizing literature in the name of record keeping, about confirming only that the book was read and understood at a very minimal level? If the key to the AR program is the point system, then what does this say about what it means to comprehend a book?" (p. 4).

"A research question worth exploring asks if the design of Accelerated Reader has an effect on children's meaning-making strategies over the long and short terms" (p. 5).

> Labbo, L. D. (1999, November). Questions worth asking about the Accelerated Reader: A response to Topping. Available at www.readingonline.org/critical/labbo/

To Literacy Coaches, Workshop Providers, and Administrators

I hope you'll check out the article by Linda Labbo on AR. This article is one of the richest and most comprehensive I've ever encountered on the subject. It examines not only the research but all the facets of reading that may be ignored if we begin to define reading as performance on tests.

---

4. Frills, gimmicks, and external rewards are temporary. Students need to be internally motivated to read and to establish a lifelong disposition toward that goal.

The following quote is from the federally sponsored book *The Voice of Evidence in Reading Research*:

"The term 'motivate' does not point to mere frills, fun, or transitory excitement, but to a cognitive commitment to learning to read and extending one's aesthetic experience. Motivation then is not isolated from the language or cognitive processes of reading, but gives energy and direction to them" (p. 329).

Guthrie, J. T., and Humenick, N. M. (2004). Motivating students to read: Evidence for classroom practices that increase reading motivation and achievement. In P. McCardle & V. Chhabra (Eds.), *The voice of evidence in reading research* (pp. 329 – 354). Baltimore, MD: Brookes Publishing.

5. **Programs such as AR and basal series that require students to complete low-level comprehension questions train students to skim the text and to concentrate on trivial details rather than to engage with the story as a whole. For more information, see:**

Kohn, A. (1999). *Punished by rewards: The trouble with gold stars, incentive plans, A's, praise, and other bribes.* New York: Houghton Mifflin.

A Final Thought

Instead of rewarding kids *because* they read, why not reward kids by *letting* them read? Why not turn the usual approach on its head? In other words, instead of saying, "You *must* read for 30 minutes every day or no recess," try saying, "Look, if we get all our work done, maybe I can allow you to have five extra minutes of reading today!" What can it hurt? Doesn't it send a more positive message than "Reading is so boring and is such hard work, I'll give you a bribe to do it" or "If you don't behave, I'll punish you by forcing you to read—or write"?

To Literacy Coaches, Workshop Providers, and Administrators

Here's a little parable Alfie Kohn tells in *Punished by Rewards: The Trouble with Gold Stars, Incentive Plans, A's, Praise, and Other Bribes* that is well worth using in workshops. Discuss it. What is its moral? How does it apply to AR and other programs that focus on external rewards? Teachers, you may want to use it when you talk to parents.

> An elderly man has endured the insults of a crowd of ten-year-olds each day as they passed his house on their way home from school. One afternoon, after listening to another round of jeers about how stupid and ugly and bald he was, the man came up with a plan. He met the children on his lawn the following Monday and announced that anyone who came back the next day and yelled rude comments about him would receive a dollar. Amazed and excited, they showed up even earlier on Tuesday, hollering epithets for all they were worth. True to his word, the old man ambled out and paid everyone. "Do the same tomorrow," he told them, "and you'll get twenty-five cents for your trouble." The kids thought that was still pretty good and turned out again on Wednesday to taunt him. At the first catcall, he walked over with a roll of quarters and again paid off his hecklers. "From now on," he announced, "I can give you only a penny for doing this." The kids looked at each other in disbelief. "A penny?" they repeated scornfully. "Forget it!" And they never came back again (pp. 71 – 72).

Kohn, A. (1999). *Punished by rewards: The trouble with gold stars, incentive plans, A's, praise, and other bribes*. New York: Houghton Mifflin.

9
Phonics: A Definition

The Tough Question

"I hear a lot about how important phonics is. What is phonics and what does it have to do with reading?"

Your Bottom-Line Answer

You Can Say: The National Reading Panel states that phonics is the connection between letters and sounds and how we use those sounds and letters in reading, writing, and spelling. We teach children phonics when they're first learning to read so they realize that the letters on the page come together to form words. There are many tools that help students learn to read. Phonics is just one of them. It can help some students some of the time.

However, the federal government's research shows that phonics has been given too much attention at the expense of other methods. Here is a direct quote from the federal government's *Report of the National Reading Panel*:

"Phonics is but a tool. A means to an end . . . . Phonics instruction that focus[es] too much on the teaching of letter-sounds and not enough on putting them to use is unlikely to be effective" (p. 2-97).

Therefore, I teach phonics sensibly, as research says I should. I balance direct instruction of phonics skills with meaningful, thoughtful application. Traditionally, most reading programs teach phonics sounds first. Using what's known as *direct instruction*, the letter sounds are specifically identified as in "This is the letter *a*. Its sound is . . . ." Children then practice the sounds in isolation. I teach letter sounds in context—instead of in isolation—so my students have enough practice in *putting them to use*—as the research says I should. I do this in a variety of ways:

◆ I teach consonant sounds first and put the most emphasis on them as we go back into a big book after reading the story, because consonant sounds tend to be more regular than vowels and are more prominent in text. Research shows that vowel sounds are "rampantly irregular." For example, more often than not the letter *a* does not make the sound in *apple*. I'll bet you can make a whole list of sounds *a* makes besides *a* in *apple*. By focusing on consonant sounds first, I make it easier for children to read and gain confidence in their abilities.

◆ When I first started teaching and followed the reading series very closely, I found I was spending too much time explaining complicated phonics rules and all the many exceptions. Research shows that teaching all those phonics rules (and exceptions) doesn't work, so I stopped doing it. I focus on a few consistent patterns and I always teach them in context. The context gives my direct instruction an extra boost.

- I use big books and enlarged text so my students can "see," as well as hear, phonics. After we've read the text together, I go back into the story and directly teach the phonics skills we need.

- I also use the context of shared writing and have the students help me sound out the words as I write on chart paper or an overhead. Then, I go back to those shared texts and directly teach phonics sounds.

By teaching phonics in context, I am applying the most scientific research methods, making the best use of instructional time, and saving money, too. Those commercial workbooks, worksheets, and phonics programs are expensive. Research cautions against placing too heavy an emphasis on phonics. This is because while phonics serves a purpose in beginning reading instruction, there are also many drawbacks to consider:

- The English language is not phonically regular. Often there are no rules to dictate when and where a particular letter or combination of letters will make a particular sound. There's no rule, for example, governing how the letters *ou* will sound in different contexts. And even when there are rules, there are often many exceptions to them. I have found that I make more efficient use of my valuable instructional time by giving my students lots of exposure to text. Research confirms that students come to recognize words on sight and internalize—just naturally memorize—phonics patterns through exposure. I balance exposure to text with direct instruction of phonics sounds in context, which helps students not just in reading but in writing as well.

- Too much emphasis on isolated phonics can discriminate against students whose first language is not English. Phonics is based on pronunciation. And pronunciation is not standard. It varies from person to person and from region to region. Not only do English language learners and students with varying dialects pronounce words differently, they can't even distinguish between certain sounds that I'm pronouncing when I'm teaching phonics. The research of the National Reading Panel warns that putting too much emphasis on phonics is particularly harmful to these students.

Something for You to Think and Talk About

I learned a lot about phonics instruction by reading and analyzing *The Report of the National Reading Panel*. What the NRP did was pull a lot of the research in the field of reading together and look at the overall results across studies. The report confirmed for me a lot of what I knew instinctively and had learned through the work of other researchers.

What I found surprising was how adamant the panel was that phonics should not be overemphasized and how strongly it warned against using commercial reading and phonics programs. The panel really stressed the role of the teacher as a decision maker as well as the personalization of instruction as opposed to standardized, tightly sequenced skills instruction or even scripts. The quotes I've cited throughout this book thus far confirm that.

I was also struck by the NRP's warnings about teaching phonics to English language learners and children with dialects that are different than the teacher's. I didn't know, for example, that we hear sounds according to the categorization of phonemes in our brains when we first learned language. That is why people speaking a language other than the one they learned when they learned to talk often speak with accents. They literally do not hear the sounds the way a native speaker pronounces them because of these phonemic categories that were imprinted on their brains when they first learned to speak.

For example, people whose first language is Japanese or Chinese often have difficulty hearing and articulating the sound of the letter *l*. It comes out sounding like an *r* because that's what they hear. Spanish speakers hear the *sh* and *ch* sounds of *shop* and *chop* as being the same sound. In such cases, "the speaker either fails to notice the difference or perceives it as a slightly different way of pronouncing the same word" (p. 2-32).

Think of the profound implications this research has for teaching phonics in our classrooms. We may well be articulating sounds that our students can't even hear! This, then, is all the more reason to teach phonics in a meaningful *context*. At least that way, the students aren't relying totally on what they hear but can *see* how those sounds and letter patterns are grounded in real text.

If the purpose of phonics is to help students with reading and writing, do commercial phonics programs, with their standardized and tightly *sequenced series* of skills, fulfill that need? Do we ever go through the prescribed sequence of skills in such programs and teach phonics to students who can already read?

The Proof

1. **_The Report of the National Reading Panel_ defines phonics in terms of function. Teachers need to emphasize the authentic application of phonics in their instruction.**

"_Phonics instruction is a way of teaching reading that stresses the acquisition of letter-sound correspondences and their use in reading and spelling. The primary focus of phonics instruction is to help beginning readers understand how letters are linked to sounds (phonemes) to form letter-sound correspondences and to help them learn how to apply this knowledge in their reading_" (p. 8).

> National Institute of Child Health and Human Development. (2000). _The report of the National Reading Panel: Summary booklet._ Washington, DC: U.S. Government Printing Office. The report can be accessed and obtained free at www.nationalreadingpanel.org

2. **According to the NRP, the _only_ purpose for phonics is to help students read and write. Instruction should focus on the purpose, rather than teaching isolated sounds.**

"_[Phonics is] a means to an end . . . . In implementing systematic phonics instruction, educators must keep the end in mind and ensure that children understand the purpose of learning letter sounds and that they are able to apply these skills . . . . in their daily reading and writing activities_" (p. 10).

> National Institute of Child Health and Human Development. (2000). _The report of the National Reading Panel: Summary booklet._ Washington, DC: U.S. Government Printing Office.

"_Phonics instruction that focus[es] too much on the teaching of letter-sounds and not enough on putting them to use are unlikely to be effective_" (p. 2-97).

> National Institute of Child Health and Human Development. (2000). _The report of the National Reading Panel: Report of the subgroups_ Washington, DC: U.S. Government Printing Office. The report can be accessed and obtained free at www.nationalreadingpanel.org

3. Students who are English language learners or who speak a dialect different from the teacher's often can't hear the differences in sounds because their brains were programmed in the sounds of their original language.

"The problem here is that phonemes in English may not be phonemes in ESL students' first language . . . . To perceive phonemes, speakers use categories that were constructed in their minds when they learned their particular language" (p. 2-41).

National Institute of Child Health and Human Development. (2000). *The report of the National Reading Panel: Report of the subgroups.* Washington, DC: U.S. Government Printing Office.

"If teachers have students who are learning English as a second language, they need to realize that their students are almost bound to misperceive some English phonemes because their linguistic minds are programmed to categorize phonemes in their first language, and this system may conflict with the phoneme categorization system in English" (p. 2-32).

National Institute of Child Health and Human Development. (2000). *The report of the National Reading Panel: Report of the subgroups.* Washington, DC: U.S. Government Printing Office.

4. English is an irregular language. Phonics is difficult to teach because there are so many variations and exceptions to the "rules."

In his seminal article, *The Utility of Phonic Generalizations in the Primary Grades,* Clymer provides a chart that lists various phonics rules/generalizations such as silent *e,* "two vowels go walking . . . ." and so on. Then he shows the percentage of utility for each—how often each generalization works.

Through Clymer's article, we not only learn what phonics patterns are worth teaching so instructional time is used most effectively, we also get a sense of how much time we spend drilling students in rules that have nearly as many exceptions as useful applications. For example, did you know that the popular "When two vowels go walking, the first one does the talking" rule only works about 45 percent of the time? In other words, it fails more often than it works, and yet I'd hate to know how much time teachers have spent teaching that as a rule or generalization and then inevitably scrambling to explain away all the exceptions. It's also interesting to read down the list and guess what degree of utility each generalization has.

It's really quite an eye opener. If you're a literacy coach or administrator, you will no doubt want to make copies of this article for your next professional development workshop. If you're a teacher, you'll want to keep this article on your desk as a guide for which phonics to stress and which to put on the back burner when you're teaching.

Clymer, T. (1963). The utility of phonic generalizations in the primary grades. *The Reading Teacher 16*, 252 – 58. This article was reprinted in 1996 in *The Reading Teacher 50*(3), 182 – 87.

The following quote is from federally sanctioned researcher Marilyn Adams, who was cited in the *2000 Politics of Education Yearbook* as one of the five most influential people in the national reading policy arena. She was also a contributor to *The Report of the National Reading Panel* and is one of the authors of the heavily phonics-focused Open Court Reading program:

"It's counterproductive to spend a lot of time teaching vowel sounds. Consonants are more likely to have a one-to-one letter sound correspondence than vowels. Vowels are 'rampantly irregular in the English writing . . . . system'" (p. 76).

Adams, M. J. (1990). *Beginning to read: Thinking and learning about print.* Cambridge, MA: Massachusetts Institute of Technology Press.

5. Phonics should be taught in context so students can make sense of it. Our best programs teach phonics in context, simultaneously with literature.

The quote below is from Timothy Shanahan, from an interview with David Boulton for the *Children of the Code* project. Shanahan is on President Bush's Literacy Panel, was a member of the National Reading Panel, and is a federally approved government researcher:

"Certainly there's a notion that, somehow, if we just teach the code, if we just teach kids the letters and what the sounds are, and teach them those entry-level skills, then everything will be fine.

"But, frankly, our best programs don't really do that. Our best programs teach those entry-level skills, but they're simultaneously introducing kids to the idea of reading; the social, meaningful aspects of reading. And so, they're dealing with comprehension or thinking with text when kids are five and six. They're doing that right along with teaching them the letter sounds and teaching them how to recognize those first words. It's not an either/or."

Shanahan, T. (2006). The personal and social implications of literacy and literacy instruction. An interview with David Boulton. It is available at www.childrenofthecode.org/interviews/shanahan.htm

6. Too much focus on isolated phonics is confusing to students because the sounds in English are so complex. The 26 letters "make over 1,100 sound-letter spelling patterns."

"But when you actually look at it, the language is much more complex than anything that we would ever try to teach. The fact is that there are many more patterns in the language, there are many more sound relationships with the letters that we don't ever get to, simply because you don't need to . . . . The best programs do not just teach the code . . . . [so that students are not] overwhelmed by the ambiguities and the false promise of consistency."

Shanahan, T. (2006). The personal and social implications of literacy and literacy instruction. An interview with David Boulton. Available at www.childrenofthecode.org/interviews/shanahan.htm

7. The problem with too much focus on isolated phonics instruction is that students perceive the galaxy of skills and sounds as pieces. Too often the focus of instruction is on the assemblage of those pieces rather than on the meaning of the text.

"[We're] standing on a mountain-top looking down [on the complexities of the phonics system and how it all fits together], but the kids are underwater."

"Instead of giving them an idea of the complexities of language, [isolated phonics instruction] gets kids set to the notion that it's absolutely consistent and easy to negotiate . . . . We teach them that it is straightforward and simple . . . . which sets them up for more failure and more shame."

Shanahan, T. (2006). The personal and social implications of literacy and literacy instruction. An interview with David Boulton. Available at www.childrenofthecode.org/interviews/shanahan.htm

For a detailed explanation of the findings of the NRP on phonics, see my two other books:

Garan, E. M. (2004). *In defense of our children: When politics, profit and education collide.* Portsmouth, NH: Heinemann.

Garan, E. M. (2001). *Resisting reading mandates: How to triumph with the truth.* Portsmouth, NH: Heinemann.

10
Phonics for Older Students

The Tough Question

When my daughter was in first grade she received a lot of phonics instruction and brought home many phonics worksheets. Now that she's older, I don't see that she's getting any phonics instruction at all from you, even though she still struggles with reading. Isn't phonics the most important skill for students to know in order to read well?

Your Bottom-Line Answer

You Can Say: The federal government's research shows that phonics instruction *does not help students above first grade with reading and spelling.* Research also warns against teaching phonics to English language learners and students with dialects that are different from the teacher's.

I still teach phonics, but I don't stress it as much as teachers in the primary grades do. I keep in mind that the research shows that there are many other important skills that are necessary for reading instruction and that I should use a variety of methods. There is no one way to teach reading. Since your daughter had a lot of phonics instruction early on in her schooling, it's possible that she just can't learn through that method.

It's also possible that she had so much phonics that she thinks reading is about saying sounds and pronouncing words instead of about getting meaning from the print. Another fact that is not widely understood is that phonics is actually learned as a result of reading—instead of through direct instruction alone. In other words, through lots of time with "eyes on text" and because I point out letter patterns through students' journal writing as well as other shared experiences, students internalize letter patterns and sounds. Research shows this to be true.

On the other hand, it could very well be that your daughter didn't get enough time with "eyes on text" or meaningful reading experiences, and that's why direct, isolated phonics instruction didn't help her. I'm filling that gap for your daughter as well as for my other struggling readers by offering lots of exposure to text. The readers who are not struggling and who are already reading quite well do not need phonics instruction, obviously, since the National Reading Panel tells us that phonics is simply a tool, a means to an end.

Also, I've known many students who don't do well with phonics but who quickly learn words by sight, without sounding them out at all. In fact, there have been periods in the history of reading in which phonics was not emphasized. Instead, the focus was on having students memorize words, often on flash cards, before they encountered those words in a story. Many people learned to read this way, and in fact the *sight word* approach was part of the famous Fun with Dick and Jane reading series.

Some students learned to read with that method, some didn't. It's the same with phonics. It helps some students. It confuses others. Too much of a stress on sounds of words can actually stop students from thinking about the meaning of the print. If your child could learn well from phonics, she wouldn't be struggling now since she had so much of it early on. I wouldn't be doing my job if I kept pushing a method on your child that didn't work for her in the past. Instead, it is my job to find out what *does* work.

And so I do what the federal government's research advises. I use a variety of teaching approaches so that those students who learn best through methods other than phonics are not left behind

Something for You to Think and Talk About

I think it's fascinating how much of the discourse on education policy is framed in terms of dichotomies—either this *or* that. The controversy over phonics is no exception. Teachers and researchers who recognize and caution about the limitations of phonics instruction are often interpreted as being anti-phonics. What the research shows us clearly is that the question is not *if* we should teach phonics but *when* and *how* we should teach it. How much is too much? When does an overemphasis on phonics and isolated skills instruction interfere with comprehension? When do we become so tangled in the pieces that we can't see the big picture? This can be true not just for students, but for teachers, too.

I hope you'll consider that it's possible for teachers to become preoccupied with isolated phonics sounds and rules—if for no other reason than that once we start, there is virtually no stopping point! There are dozens and dozens of sounds and generalizations and exceptions. So it's easy to get lost in that minutiae and forget to stand back and reflect on what messages about reading we are communicating to students. If children spend way more time on phonics than on actually reading, then you can see how they would get the impression that learning phonics is the goal rather than a tool for meaning making.

Students learn what we teach them. If we teach them pieces of language, they will learn pieces of language. If we test them on those isolated skills we taught them, they will perform all right, but those skills do not necessarily transfer to comprehension. The research clearly shows this.

I find something else intriguing. The idea that students must learn phonics to read is so deeply ingrained in some educators that they find it impossible to even consider that maybe the famous fourth-grade slump is because of an overemphasis on phonics. That slump comes when more demands are put on students, when they are no longer demonstrating their reading proficiency by filling in blanks on phonics worksheets with isolated sounds. There comes a time when they stop learning to read through skills production and they need to demonstrate that they can read to learn.

This has been true historically, and it remains true today. There's a baffling inclination in education to keep pushing more of what didn't work in the first place—from isolated phonics to formal grammar instruction to more homework to making the school day longer—even though there is no research to support any of those solutions. That is something I hope you'll think about.

Here's a quote that puts in perspective the practice of drilling and then testing students in isolated skills. It's from a position statement published by the International Reading Association:

> "What do we mean when we say a method works? In some studies a method works if children are able to read lists of words in isolation. In others 'works' means that children can answer questions on a multiple-choice test. If there is anything we have learned from methods studies, it is that children learn what we teach them (Pearson & Fielding, 1991). If we teach them how to pronounce pseudowords, they learn how to pronounce pseudowords and sometimes lists of regular words. If we teach children to summarize, they learn how to give better summaries. Therefore, many methods have a right to claim they 'work,' but that does not necessarily mean that any of these methods are better than all or most other methods or that any one of them is the 'right' method. For all these reasons beginning reading instruction has been controversial" (p. 3).

International Reading Association. (1999). Using multiple methods of beginning reading instruction: A position statement of the International Reading Association.

So, here's something to think about: Whether a method works or not depends on how we measure success. And how we measure success is contingent on how we define *reading*. A focus on isolated skills instruction can give the illusion of success if that's all we measure. I'm hoping we can frame the discussion of phonics by talking not about *if*, but about *how, when,* and *how much* we teach it.

What is often lost in heavily skills-focused reading programs is the importance of the *act* and ultimate *purpose* of reading. Furthermore, such programs tend to ignore the research proving the importance of immersing kids in a literate environment and the fact that many skills are learned through such exposure. There is no real dispute among researchers that children who are read to become better readers than those who are not read to. Researchers have hypothesized about the reasons for this powerful phenomenon and believe that children's early exposure to print—sitting on a parent's lap as they are being read to, for example—provides a basic sense of written language, how story works, as opposed to the less formal structures of spoken language. That makes sense.

Researchers also believe that immersion in and familiarity with print allows students to absorb important print conventions, including phonics, punctuation, and word recognition. That is, with no direct instruction, children learn a lot about print, including a sense of phonics and the alphabetic principle. It is this research-based recognition of the importance of print immersion, of course, that inspired the use of big books and enlarged print in classrooms. That way, teachers replicate the at-home, lap-book experience that some children may have missed. We can't just ignore the research-proven fact that some skills are sometimes "caught" through immersion in print and literature rather than "taught" through direct skills instruction. In fact, *The Report of the National Reading Panel* acknowledges that students acquire skills such as phonics and other print conventions incidentally.

Sometimes I read something that just rings true. I want to end here with a very provocative quote by teacher and author Regie Routman that really struck me. Whether you agree with it or not, it will get you thinking. Regie is not a federally approved researcher. She is a teacher who reflects on and articulates her own classroom experiences. Regie puts into words what you have probably experienced and research has shown to be true.

> *"It has become crystal clear to me that children learn phonics best after they can already read. I am convinced that the reason our good readers are good at phonics is that in their being able to read they can intuitively make sense of phonics. When phonics is isolated as the main method of teaching, students are prevented from utilizing natural meaningful processes. Reading is then viewed as a word-by-word process which is quite inefficient, nonsensical, and frustrating"* (p. 44).

Routman, R. (1988). *Transitions*. Portsmouth, NH: Heinemann.

I'm not suggesting that teachers abandon direct instruction. I'm suggesting that they implement direct instruction *after* exposing students to the text. You can still introduce the specific skill or sound directly, and you can still give students practice by writing words with the letter patterns you are teaching on whiteboards or on chart paper. Use a phonics checklist if you like, so that you are teaching sequentially as well as opportunistically. This way, you cover all bases. We can use direct instruction and provide students with the added bonus of seeing how the skill works in real reading. Nothing is sacrificed. We can help students internalize phonics naturally, reading real text with a direct instruction boost. Or vice versa— we can teach skills explicitly with a boost of contextual reading.

The Proof

1. The NRP Report, the federal government's gold standard for reading research, found that phonics instruction did not benefit the reading of students above first grade.

The following quotes are from the report:

"[As a result of phonics instruction,] comprehension of text was not significantly improved for 'older students' (above first grade)" (p. 9).

"Systematic phonics instruction failed to exert a significant impact on the reading performance of low-achieving readers in 2nd through 6th grade" (p. 88).

"Phonics instruction appears to contribute only weakly, if at all, in helping poor readers apply these (decoding skills) to read text and to spell words" (p. 108).

National Institute of Child Health and Human Development. (2000). *The report of the National Reading Panel: Report of the subgroups (comprehension)*. Washington, DC: U.S. Government Printing Office. The report can be accessed and obtained free at www.nationalreadingpanel.org

2. Phonics should not be overemphasized. There is no one way to teach reading. Teachers need to balance instruction and use a variety of methods.

The quote below is by Open Court author Marilyn Adams, who was cited in the 2000 *Politics of Education Yearbook* as one of the five most influential people in the national reading policy arena:

"Given the tremendous variations from school to school and implementation to implementation, we should be very clear that the prescription of a method can never in itself guarantee the best of all possible outcomes" (pp. 38–39).

> Adams, M. J. (1990). *Beginning to read: Thinking and learning about print.* Cambridge, MA: MIT Press.

This next quote is by Linnea Ehri, who was the chair of the Alphabetics Committee for the NRP report:

"[The report did not] single out any one way to teach reading. Rather, multiple ways were found to be effective" (p. 4).

> Ehri, L. C. (2001, June/July). National Reading Panel Report: Work praised, but distortion fears persist [Interview]. *Reading Today.*

Jay Samuels, who was also a member of the National Reading Panel, states:

"Many of our educational pundits appear to believe there are universal approaches to instruction and development of curricular materials which will work for all children under all conditions . . . . Depending on these variables as well as the degree of motivation and prior knowledge brought to the task of learning to read, it is highly likely that some approaches to instruction should be better for some children and different approaches should work better for other children" (p. 390).

> Samuels, S. J. (1984). Editorial. *Reading Research Quarterly, 19,* 390 – 92.

3. Students can learn skills naturally (incidentally) when they are immersed in print.

The following quote is from *The Report of the National Reading Panel*:

"It is important to recognize that children will acquire phonemic awareness and phonics in the course of learning to read and spell even though they are not taught PA explicitly" (p. 2-43).

> National Institute of Child Health and Human Development. (2000). *The report of the National Reading Panel: Report of the subgroups.* Washington, DC: U.S. Government Printing Office.

4. **Reading instruction should not begin with the skill. It is most effective when it begins with meaning and when phonics is taught simultaneously with comprehension.**

The quote below is by Timothy Shanahan, who is on President Bush's Literacy Panel, was a member of the National Reading Panel, and is a federally approved government researcher:

"If we're talking about teaching here, certainly one fundamental notion that would need to be stressed is how complex literacy is. Frankly, it's that complexity that you have to introduce to kids. It's not, 'We'll work up to the complexity.' We actually start there" (p. 14).

> Shanahan, T. (2006). The personal and social implications of literacy and literacy instruction. An interview with David Boulton. Available at www.childrenofthecode.org/interviews/shanahan.htm

11
Phonemic Awareness

The Tough Question

"*When I was in school, I was never taught phonemic awareness, and yet I learned to read. What is it and what does it have to do with learning to read?*"

Your Bottom-Line Answer

You Can Say: Phonemic awareness (PA) is the ability to manipulate—to segment and blend—the sounds of spoken language. A phoneme is the smallest unit of sound in spoken language.

Phonemic awareness can help students to sound out words. Of course, not all reading is based on sounding out words. In fact, sometimes students read words in one giant gulp instead of one sound and letter at a time. Therefore, the federal government's research warns against too much emphasis on phonemic awareness. In fact, as little as five hours of training a year is more effective than programs that use more than eighteen hours of training in a year.

Perhaps one of the most important uses of phonemic awareness is in connection with children's early attempts at writing. Children shape the phonemes with their mouths as they translate the letters on the page. For this reason, the federal government's *Report of the National Reading Panel* states that phonemic awareness is best taught as it is used—with letters in situations that model how it is used in reading and writing. I diligently apply the research recommendations of the National Reading Panel in teaching phonemic awareness.

- I teach PA with letters by having students help me sound out the words as I write on an overhead or chart paper. In this way they see how the phonemes match the letters on the page. They are also seeing a model of what they need to do when they are writing.

- By using the research in my classroom and teaching PA in context by modeling writing, I'm not just showing students the sound-letter matches. I'm also helping them to get a grasp of the sound-letter mismatches, since English is not a phonetically regular language. One phoneme does not match one letter. For example, the long-*e* phoneme requires more than one letter to form it. Actually, there are several combinations of letters that form long *e*, such as *ea*, *ee*, *ei*, and *ie*. By modeling writing with my students, I am showing and telling them the tricks of English phonics and spelling.

- I expose my students to lots of reading and writing because the research shows that they learn phonemic awareness as well as phonics just from lots of exposure to print.

Commercial phonemic awareness or phonics programs are very expensive. It is *your* tax money that pays for them. Luckily, the research shows they are not necessary! I save you money by modeling skills in real reading and writing situations just as the research says I should.

This means more work for me than if I used some expensive commercial program, but it is my job to work hard, apply the research, and save money by doing what's best for my students.

Something for You to Think and Talk About

The National Reading Panel itself says that PA and other skills should be defined in terms of their function—they serve a purpose in literacy. They are not the goal of literacy and should be kept in perspective. The NRP report clearly and unambiguously states, "PA instruction was more effective when it was taught with letters. Using letters with phonemes helps children make the transfer to reading and writing" (p. 2-133). Thus, engaging students in shared writing as they help us sound out words meets this criteria.

In spite of the federal government's own recommendations, though, there is a puzzling distortion and misrepresentation of the NRP's findings. For example, some phonics programs focus on teaching PA all by itself—just pulling apart and putting together sounds or using picture cards or words devoid of context. Such practices run counter to the scientific research.

Here's something else to think about. We know that learning, especially learning for young children, should be concrete. We know they do not grasp abstractions easily. When we break up language into small pieces that are no longer recognizable as language, are we making the instruction more concrete or are we making it abstract? When we take those pieces, be they phonemes or phonics patterns, and remove them from how they are really used and teach them in isolation, are we making it easier or harder for students to grasp why the skills are taught and how they are to apply them?

The other idea I'd like you to think about may surprise you. I suggest that you spend more time on PA than the five to eighteen hours that the NRP report recommends. But not doing direct, isolated skills instruction. What's important to keep in mind is that the studies the NRP discusses looked at that kind of instruction and found that a little goes a long way. However, when we look at how the NRP says PA should be taught—in context by modeling how it's applied in reading and especially writing—then the amount we should teach dramatically increases. In other words, if you have your students help you do lots of writing, if you model how we blend and segment sounds, and if you have students play with words by singing silly songs and reading lots of poems, then I think you'll find you far exceed the amount of direct instruction the NRP recommends.

Again, I want to emphasize that by teaching skills in context you are not sacrificing anything. You are doing more—not less—than programs that use only direct instruction of isolated skills. You are adding a research-proven dimension to the abstract and *confusing* out-of-context instruction that so much of our teaching sometimes gets reduced to.

The Proof

1. Phonemic awareness should be taught as it is used—with letters, in context.

Students should be exposed to activities that model manipulating phonemes with letters because doing so "help[s] children make the connection between PA and its application to reading [and writing]" (p. 2-41).

> National Institute of Child Health and Human Development. (2000). *The report of the National Reading Panel: Report of the subgroups (phonemic awareness).* Washington, DC: U.S. Government Printing Office. The report can be accessed and obtained free at www.nationalreadingpanel.org

2. Teachers do not need to spend more than a few minutes a day on direct instruction of phonemic awareness.

The optimum amount of time for direct PA instruction is only five to eighteen hours a year. "These findings suggest that PA instruction does not need to be lengthy to exert its strongest effect on spelling and reading" (p. 2-41).

> National Institute of Child Health and Human Development. (2000). *The report of the National Reading Panel: Report of the subgroups (phonemic awareness).* Washington, DC: U.S. Government Printing Office.

3. The NRP report confirms that, like phonics, PA can be learned just through exposure to text—without explicit, direct instruction.

"It is important to recognize that children will acquire phonemic awareness in the course of learning to read and spell even though they are not taught PA explicitly" (p. 2-43).

National Institute of Child Health and Human Development. (2000). *The report of the National Reading Panel: Report of the subgroups (phonemic awareness)*. Washington, DC: U.S. Government Printing Office.

A Final Thought

The role of phonics and other skills instruction is a controversial issue, and controversy makes us uncomfortable. In fact, it makes me uncomfortable. However, how can we answer tough questions about teaching or, more importantly, become better teachers without coming to terms with the difficult issues that lurk behind the questions that teachers are asked and the materials and methods we are required to use?

12

The Cueing Systems and Eye-Movement Research

The Tough Question

" How do you make sure my son reads every letter and every word? When he reads out loud at home, sometimes he misses words, so I'm afraid he might not be noticing all the letters and words when he reads. Or worse yet, I think he uses the meaning of the sentence to help him guess some words instead of sounding them out. "

Your Bottom-Line Answer

You Can Say: Scientific research shows that struggling readers focus on every word or even every letter. Good readers do not. I teach the strategies that good readers use instead of training my students in unsuccessful methods.

Thanks to the newest, most innovative technology, we can see exactly what the eyes do during reading. We can see where the eyes stop or *fixate* and how they track print. And what we've learned is that good readers do not read every word, much less every letter. When they hit a troubling word, they stop or fixate for a moment. Then they reread. They go back to the sentence they've just read to cross-check. They use the context to *double-check* the word. It's really very smart.

This is what researchers and surveyors do. They make sure their assessments and data are correct. They don't accept their first conclusion. They confirm by cross-checking using a method called *triangulation*—making sure that all the data lead to the same, correct conclusion. We don't consciously triangulate when we read, but we do it subtly when we make an error—a *miscue*.

And how do we know if we've miscued? We recognize that the word we've read doesn't sound right or doesn't make sense in the sentence. The context, the *meaning*—or what's called *semantics*—often signals to us that we've made an error.

To Literacy Coaches, Workshop Providers, and Administrators

Here is a demonstration you can use in workshops that shows we do not read letter by letter or even word by word. All of us sometimes make errors when we read. When that happens, we get a jolt because a word doesn't make sense. Pay attention to what you do and I'll bet you'll see that you go back, reread the sentence, and then look more carefully at the letters in the word that threw you. You triangulate. You use the context (the meaning or semantics), you use the grammatical structure of the sentence (the *syntax* or the *structure* of the sentence), and then you go back and more carefully look at the letters or the word—the *visual*, or *graphophonemic*, clues.

Put the following three sentences on overhead transparencies. Cover them with sheets of paper. Ask the audience to read with you as you move the paper. For sentence #1, move the paper so one letter at a time is revealed. For sentence #2, move the paper so one word at a time is revealed. For sentence #3, uncover the entire sentence so the audience has the context to support their reading of it.

1. See how hard it is to read letter by letter.

2. Reading by whole words is somewhat less stressful.

3. When you have the entire text to provide context, reading is much easier because you see now that we do not read every word, much less every letter.

Now ask your workshop participants, was reading sentence #1 one letter at a time easy or hard? What does that tell us about putting too much focus on individual letters when we teach reading?

Was reading sentence #2 one word at a time a little easier than when we focused on individual letters? By the way, did you think the last word would be different than what it was? Did you anticipate that the word would be *difficult* instead of *stressful*? That was your sense of meaning and language cueing you. What signaled the miscue was your use of the visual or *graphophonemic* cue/clue—seeing the word *stressful* revealed. How did reading sentence #3 compare to reading sentence #1 and sentence #2?

As teachers, our goal is to make students successful. Therefore, why would I stress reading letter by letter or word by word when that makes reading harder, as we've seen in this demonstration?

All three of the cueing systems—meaning/semantic, syntax/sentence structure, visual/graphophonemic-work together for good readers. When good readers are jolted by a miscue or unexpected word in a sentence, they reread and cross-check with more emphasis on one of the other cues/clues.

The cueing systems, then, are derived from the knowledge of how language works. Good readers know that not just any old word will do and that all the evidence in a sentence must triangulate and reach the right conclusion. Struggling readers do not have an awareness of how language works to help them when they miscue. Often they think reading is all about the letters or all about saying the words. They are lost when they make a mistake because there is no cue—no clue, no red flag—to *jolt* them into getting that word right. Furthermore, eye-movement research shows us that struggling readers are far more likely to focus on every letter or every word than are good readers, who read in meaningful phrases.

Here's more proof that reading letter by letter or even word by word isn't helpful and that we need the context of the sentence to help us read. Many words have no meaning—and in fact can't even be pronounced—without context. For example, try to pronounce the following: bow-bow read-read.

There's no way you can know you are pronouncing those words correctly unless they are in a sentence. All the phonics in the world will not help. You need the meaning, the semantics, to help you read those words. They are just a bunch of letters when we yank them out of a sentence.

> Researchers have known for decades that we don't read—or we *shouldn't* read—letter by letter or word by word. However, now the latest technology gives us undeniable proof that this is so. I use this research to inform the way I teach reading.

Something for You to Think and Talk About

I have a couple of thoughts here that I'd like to share with you. One is how "sound it out" is sometimes an automatic response when helping students read. For example, I've heard student teachers say, "Sound it out"— automatically— when a student is stuck on a word such as *once* without realizing that it can't be sounded out. Or consider the word *mother*. Is it *moth* with an *er* sound attached? Or *father*. Is that sounded out as *fat + her*? And yes, I do know that those are sight words and are taught as such, but I'm suggesting that in terms of application, in terms of offering appropriate help and interventions, sometimes "sound it out" is used automatically instead of appropriately.

I'm also hoping that you'll think about the language that you use when discussing your practices. If you're a literacy coach or administrator, why not take a minute and learn the names of some of the researchers I've mentioned or write them on note cards or overheads when you present a workshop? I understand that it's not practical to go back and read every study but you can make yourself a more credible and powerful professional by naming some of the studies. If you are a teacher, then it can't hurt to mention the research when talking to parents or administrators. The researchers and even the background of the studies are right here at your fingertips. I hope you'll acquire and use that language.

There's one other talking/thinking point to consider about the professional language we use. There are parents, journalists, and even some researchers who are confused by the idea that good readers use all the cueing systems. It is their belief that if graphophonemics is mastered, then context and syntax cues are irrelevant. I believe that the use of the phrase *guessing at words* adds to this confusion. It insinuates that by having students cross-check by using context, we're telling them to throw a dart at some mental word wall and that any word they hit is just as good as any other. Actually, we're doing just the opposite!

In point of fact, what we're saying is, "Look, whatever word you read has to make sense in that sentence. It's not good enough for you to toss in whatever strikes your fancy. If it doesn't make sense, go back and read it again more carefully."

Instead of saying that you're teaching students to "guess words," consider using language such as "I teach my students to cross-check for meaning. I teach them to *triangulate* and *cross-check for accuracy* instead of relying on just one narrow, really limited approach to word identification." On a more positive note, I do hope that you will cite the scientific technology and the laser videos of the newest eye-movement research. Why not show off a little?

The Proof

1. **The latest eye-movement videos use laser points to track what the eyes of good readers do as they read authentic, connected text. The videos prove that good readers make fewer fixations than poor readers. Good readers "read" (fixate on) only about 67 percent of the words in a sentence. This means they do not read word by word.**

To Literacy Coaches, Workshop Providers, and Administrators

I want to recommend an absolutely stunning little book. It's easy to read, and it has many, many examples of eye movements on authentic, connected texts. You can put the examples on overheads and use them in workshops. I have. And what's best, all the research in this book is absolutely scientific. There are other helpful quotes in this section that would also make good overheads and talking points for workshops. Teachers, the examples in the following book helped clarify for me how we use the cueing systems:

Paulson, E. J., & Freeman, A. E. (2003). *Insight from the eyes: The science of effective reading instruction.* Portsmouth, NH: Heinemann.

See also:
Duckett, P. (2002). New insights: Eye fixations and the reading process. *Talking Points, 13*(2), 16 – 21.

2. **Good readers use the surrounding words—the context—of a sentence to identify words.**

The following quote is from an interview with eye-movement researcher Keith Rayner and is available online. It is important because Rayner's work has been misinterpreted as evidence that we read word by word or even letter by letter.

He does not say that at all. Rayner does believe that students need phonics instruction and that graphophonemics is important in learning to read. However, he also recognizes that good readers use context (the meaning or semantic cueing system), which makes reading more efficient and accurate.

"So before you get to a word, before the eyes actually fixate on it, there's a preview benefit; you get some facilitation of the upcoming word . . . . Letter-by-letter reading [is] literally very hard."

> Rayner, K. (2004, March). What eye movements tell us about the processing involved in reading. This interview is available online at www.childrenofthecode.org/interviews/rayner.htm

3. We skip words when we read. The more predictable the word, the more likely we are to skip it. Thus, we "sample" text. We use the context of the text to derive meaning. We do *not* focus on every word.

"The predictability of a word (or the amount of contextual constraint for that word) . . . . will affect both fixation time and word skipping" (p. 507).

> Rayner, K., & Well, A.D. (1996). Effects of contextual constraint on eye movements in reading: A further examination. *Psychonomic Bulletin & Review, 3*(4), 504 – 509.

4. Readers do "reruns," or regressions, when they are struck by text that is ambiguous or confusing, or when they have miscued on a word. Thus, they confirm or disprove their initial response by refocusing their attention on the semantic and syntactic cueing systems—the context.

"Regressive fixations usually are launched to areas of the text that have caused linguistic confusion, or contain particularly complicated words" (p. 146).

> Underwood, G., & Batt, V. (1996). *Reading and understanding.* Oxford: Blackwell Publishing.

Note: You can find examples of readers' regressions and make overheads from them for workshops in the Paulson and Freeman book I cited on page 93.

5. Good readers are strategic in making sense of print. They sample text and use all the cueing systems to cross-check their accuracy.

The quote below is from National Reading Panel contributor Steven Stahl in *The Voice of Evidence in Reading Research:*

"Cueing children to use their knowledge of words to decode unknown words in context [is a useful strategy]" (p. 191).

> Stahl, S. (2004). What do we know about fluency? Findings of the National Reading Panel. In P. McCardle & V. Chhabra (Eds.), *The voice of evidence in reading research* (pp. 187 – 211). Baltimore, MD: Brookes Publishing.

Stahl cites Marie Clay and her work on Reading Recovery:

> Clay, M. M. (1983). *Reading recovery: A guidebook for teachers in training.* Portsmouth, NH: Heinemann.

A Final Thought

The scientific findings of the eye-movement research is very clear: reading is not a word-by-word, much less a letter-by-letter, process. Keith Rayner (who is very much from a behaviorist paradigm) and many other influential eye-movement researchers have proved as much. Incredibly, however, their work has been used as "proof" that reading *is* a letter-by-letter and word-by-word process. What's important about these misrepresentations is that they seep down into the public consciousness and are picked up by publishers who advocate for intensely skills-based instruction that ignores—and in fact may even be contemptuous of—the evidence that we use more than phonics to read. That is something to think about when you are confronted with those misrepresentations of research.

13
Decodable Text

The Tough Question

"What is 'decodable text'? I read something about it in a newspaper article that said it helps all kids read but is especially good for struggling readers because it helps them pronounce the words. My son is still struggling with reading. Do you use decodable text to help him?"

Your Bottom-Line Answer

You Can Say: *Phonics* is the relationship between letters and the sounds they make to form words. English is an alphabetic language. There is some connection between letters and spoken language. However, the English language is not phonetically regular. The sounds that letters make in isolation and in combination with other letters are not consistent. Often there are no rules to guide us as to why letters make one sound in one word and a totally different sound in another.

The inconsistencies of spelling patterns in English are confusing to students when they are learning to read. Decodable texts are designed to focus on words with consistent spelling patterns. In fact, the rule for decodable texts is that 80 to 90 percent of the words must follow the rule and use the sound being taught. The idea is that if the words in the story are controlled, and they all follow simple, limited letter patterns, and if those patterns are taught one at a time, students can immediately read the text. All they need to read a passage is knowledge of the pattern and a couple of sight words.

For example, if we teach the pattern _ig by simply changing the beginning letter, we change the word. So students can pretty easily sound out any words with that ig pattern, assuming they know their beginning consonant sounds. This is known as *teaching by analogy*. If you can read ig, you can read *pig*. If you can read *pig*, you can read *big* and *jig* and *wig*.

So a decodable text might start with a picture of a pig. The text might read: "Pig. Big pig. Big, big pig." The next page might have a picture of a pig in a wig doing a jig. The text might read: "Jig, pig. Jig, big, big pig. Jig, big, big pig in a wig." Subsequent stories in decodable texts might introduce other extremely regular phonics patterns such as *it*, *in*, and *it*.

There are some advantages to using decodable text, including the fact that young children feel success immediately because, with very little instruction, they think they can read. But there are also many disadvantages:

- The "stories" don't make sense. This gives students the idea that reading is about pronouncing words, not getting meaning from print. This is especially true if much or most of the reading students do is focused on decodable text.

- Because English is an irregular language, decodable stories with limited word patterns do not prepare students for the reality of complex text using a variety of words and spelling patterns.

- The language in decodable text is unnatural. We don't talk like that—in stilted, phonetically regular word patterns. This is a particular concern for my English language learners. I want them to pick up the flow, the rhythms, and genuine vocabulary of English by exposure to lots of meaningful context as the research says I should. Therefore, decodable text runs counter to the idea of English immersion to help students learn to speak English.

- What's more, in decodable texts, the individual words are often contrived and even dated because the people who write those stories are hunting for patterned words instead of authentic words that reflect the beauty of the English language. For example, some of those stories use words such as *chap* or *gal* or *pal* or *bam*. These are words most adults don't use anymore, much less children. Exposures to such words don't help students learn vocabulary.

- To become good readers, students must learn to use meaning—the context and sentence structure of a text—to cross-check their reading for accuracy. When we read standard text, we know when we make a mistake because the wrong word doesn't make sense when we read it. So a red flag goes up, and we go back and reread, looking at the word more carefully, and then we get it right. However, if students consistently read texts that don't make sense and use unnatural words and language, there is nothing to send up a red flag when they make an error and they don't learn this valuable reading strategy.

- The stories in decodable text are boring to the point of being insulting. Nevertheless, they are now being used with intermediate and even high school students.

Since there is no research supporting the use of decodable text, and I should use only those methods that are scientifically based, I use very little of it. On those rare occasions that I do use it, I make sure students understand that it is just for practicing sounds. I don't call it *reading* because I don't want to give students the wrong impression of what reading is. Or sometimes I may have students write "silly sentences" and then pick them out of a hat so they can learn the regular phonics patterns for reading and spelling, but I limit and qualify the use of nonsensical stories and word practice, as research recommends I should.

Something for You to Think and Talk About

What message do we send to children when we require them to read stories that don't make sense and force them to focus on pronunciation instead of meaning? How do such stories affect the self-confidence of intermediate students who are required to read about pigs doing jigs, cats in hats and "chaps" and "gals"? We need to ensure that we use reading materials that sound like English. Decodable texts almost sound like another language.

The Proof

1. **There is *no* independent research to support the use of decodable text in spite of its widespread and even required use as part of many commercial reading series.**

The following quotes are from the in-depth analysis of research on decodable text by Richard Allington and Haley Woodside-Jiron. Allington is a member of the Reading Hall of Fame and is former president of the International Reading Association. He is a respected researcher in the field of reading:

"An examination of each of the research references cited in various advocacy and policy statements as supporting the use of an instructional emphasis on 'decodable text' found that only a few research reports were cited but some were cited repeatedly" (p. 202).

"We have carefully traced the research citations noted in advocacy and policy statements and were unable to locate any 'reliable, replicable research' concerning the use of 'decodable text' on which these policy decisions were based" (p. 213).

"It is troublesome that policies and mandates [such as the use of decodable texts] that do not have a foundation in research findings can become widely accepted as being 'research based'" (p. 213).

"Recommending broad policy and sweeping mandates for reading instruction [such as the use of decodable texts] without careful attention to existing and future research that is both relevant and meaningful undermines both the development of more effective reading programs and important academic discourse" (p. 214).

Allington, R., & Woodside-Jiron, H. (2002). Decodable text in beginning reading: Are mandates and policy based on research? In R. Allington (Ed.), *Big brother and the national reading curriculum: How ideology trumped evidence* (pp. 195 – 216). Portsmouth, NH: Heinemann.

2. ***The Report of the National Reading Panel*** **acknowledges the lack of research on decodable text and does not recommend its use. Nevertheless, decodable texts are falsely touted by publishers as being "research-based."**

The quote below is from NRP's report, the federal government's gold standard for reading research:

"Very little research has attempted to determine whether the use of decodable books in systematic phonics programs has any influence on the progress that some or all children make in learning to read" (p. 2-137).

National Institute of Child Health and Human Development. (2000). *The report of the National Reading Panel: Report of the subgroups.* Washington, DC: U.S. Government Printing Office. The report can be accessed and obtained free at www.nationalreadingpanel.org

14
Fluency and Comprehension/DIBELS

The Tough Question

" In other classes the teachers use stopwatches to train students to read faster. How do you make sure my son is reading fast enough? Shouldn't you be training him to take the DIBELS fluency test that other teachers are using? "

Your Bottom-Line Answer

You Can Say: Many think that fluency is how fast a person can read. But fluency is about more than just speed. The definition of *fluency* also includes accuracy and correct phrasing. In research terminology, phrasing is known by the technical term *prosody*. However, speed, accuracy, and prosody are not enough to make a student a good reader. Research proves that fluency should not be separated from comprehension.

In fact, research proves that too much training in fluency can actually *interfere* with comprehension. My goal is to help your child be a thinker and to understand what he reads. Instead of using a stopwatch to time his reading, I keep the following research-proven facts in mind when I teach fluency:

◆ Reading is not a race. It's about making sense of the words and ideas on the page. I'm very careful about the subtle messages I communicate to my students. I don't want to give them the impression that the goal of reading is speed.

◆ There is no cruise control for smart reading. Good readers vary their speed according to the text and their needs. I want your child to slow down and think when he encounters difficult text instead of racing through it. When he's reading for pleasure, I want him to linger over the text, to savor and appreciate the story. I would be doing my students a disservice if I didn't teach them to adjust their reading speed according to the text.

Many concerns surround the fluency assessment known as DIBELS (Dynamic Indicators of Basic Literacy Skills) because the claims made on its Web site are done by people associated with DIBELS, not by independent researchers. My own experience with DIBELS, combined with a careful study of independent research findings, leads me to the following conclusions:

◆ The federal government's research proves that when kids in first grade are just beginning to read, fluency does help comprehension—up to a point. After that, too much speed can be counterproductive. Faster is not always better. The research shows that for older students, or for students who are beyond a beginning reading level, faster pronunciation of words doesn't help them become better readers.

◆ DIBELS is based on speed, and so it sends students the wrong message—that the faster they read, the better they read. However, worse than that, it does not focus students on getting meaning from connected text or even real words. Sections of the test force students to identify quickly only parts of words made up of nonsensical combinations of letters. What is the point of that? What does "reading" nonsensical sounds at breakneck speed have to do with real reading? In other words, much of DIBELS neglects an important facet of fluency—prosody, or phrasing. This process of sounding out letters and words without regard to meaning is known as *barking at print*.

◆ Using a stopwatch puts anyone—even adults—under a lot of pressure. What's the point of that? Research shows that I should teach my students to be thoughtful connoisseurs of authentic, connected print—instead of indiscriminate gobblers and chirpers of meaningless sounds. I want my students to be thoughtful and deliberate. These are rare strengths that I want to encourage, not destroy. Using a stopwatch and forcing students to race through lists of nonsensical sounds does not respect and utilize those strengths.

◆ It's possible to read with fluency, even with correct phrasing, and have virtually no idea of the text's meaning. Often this disconnect between reading speed and the ability to comprehend is the result of too much focus on reading fast. Research clearly shows that DIBELS training does not help comprehension. DIBELS's test of "comprehension" gauges the number of words a student can repeat from a passage, not her depth of understanding. Students can actually scramble words and still get a good score as long as they repeat the words that appeared in the passage. This sends a signal to students that they don't need to think about and understand that words come together to convey meaning.

◆ DIBELS discriminates against minorities, English language learners, students with regional dialects and/or speech problems, and even students who are missing teeth! This is because the test is based solely on pronunciation and speed. DIBELS actually penalizes children for having an accent or from being from a different part of the country than the teacher, no matter how well they can actually read. My job is to close the achievement gap—not widen it.

◆ Scientific studies of the brain show that people who have an accent that differs from someone else's cannot even hear, much less pronounce, sounds that differ from those in their original language or dialect. That includes teachers. Therefore, the DIBELS test makers cannot guarantee that any teacher hears and pronounces the sounds correctly herself.

◆ The newest objective studies, by federally approved researchers, show that DIBELS does not predict which students will be good readers and which will not. Nevertheless, important decisions—including whether students should repeat a grade—are sometimes made about students' futures based on DIBELS.

- ◆ I discovered yet another disturbing fact about DIBELS. The test results are sent not just to the state but to a large database in Oregon. This is too much like Big Brother for me. I believe that your child's performance in school should be confidential. So what DIBELS amounts to is a permanent record—scored and stored in a distant location—of students' temporary and meaningless performance behaviors.

- ◆ DIBELS is expensive. The test can be downloaded "free." However, the scoring costs one dollar per student. This doesn't sound like much but most students are tested more than once a year. Overall, this costs taxpayers over five million dollars per year.

When I first started teaching, I used to rush my students through reading, "Faster, faster, faster." Then I studied the research and discovered the harm that I was doing. My own experience confirms what the research shows. I have found that giving students more time for sustained silent reading—just the practice of "eyes on text"—actually helps them become more fluent than forcing them to read quickly. I also do lots of reading aloud and shared reading so that my students, especially the English language learners, become totally surrounded—marinated—in the sounds of language. Immersion in literacy is a brilliant way to help my class become better, more expressive readers at the same time they develop a love of literature.

I believe—and research confirms—that speed-reading is a hindrance instead of a help to your child. It keeps him from reaching the goal we all share for his future as an intelligent, thoughtful, lifelong reader.

Something for You to Think and Talk About

Instead of just discussing the problems the research reveals about speed-reading and the relationship between fluency and comprehension—and vice versa—I think it would be helpful if you experienced what we put our students through when we time them. The following exercise is ideal for workshops, but I think that just by reading it, you can discover for yourself that timed reading, DIBELS, and speed-reading of nonsense words do not help with comprehension.

To Literacy Coaches, Workshop Providers, and Administrators

Here is a demonstration you can do with a group of teachers. Teachers, you can do this demonstration with parents.

1. **Put the following passage on an overhead. Ask for a volunteer to read it aloud while you time her with a stopwatch. Tell the volunteer that on the second reading, she'll be expected to do it faster. Alternatively, pair up the teachers in your audience and hold the stopwatch while they take turns reading the passage:**

   This essay is a philosophical and sociological reconsideration of the nature of teaching and work. It draws broadly from the sociology of Pierre Bourdieu and materialist models of the economic subject. It begins from an acknowledgment and review of the critiques of current policy orientations to testing and accountability in the United States, Australia, and the United Kingdom. One of the principal effects is the reconstruction of the teacher as commodity fetishist. The case is made that reassertions of definitions of teaching as craft and profession are of limited value in responding to new economic and policy conditions. A proposal is made for the reenvisioning of teachers and teaching in relation to cosmopolitan, transcultural contexts and conditions (Luke, p. 1422).

   Luke, A. Teaching after the market: From commodity to cosmopolitan.
   Teachers College Record, 7(106) 1422 – 1433.

2. **After the teachers have been timed reading the passage, ask the following questions:**

   ◆ Did you read the passage fluently? Could you pretty much read every word with correct pronunciation and even correct phrasing?

   ◆ In spite of your generally fluent reading (I'm assuming) of the passage, do you have any idea what you read? Would reading it any faster than you just did help or hinder your comprehension?

   ◆ Even if you had the needed background knowledge to comprehend this passage, do you think you'd understand it better if you read it more slowly rather than faster?

◆ Did the fact that you were being timed with a stopwatch help or hinder your comprehension? Do you think the fact that you were being timed shifted your focus from meaning to speed?

3. **Put the following text on the overhead and say: "Now that you've read the passage and I've timed you, I'd like you to practice reading the following nonsense syllables as fast as you can as I time you" (Note: these nonsense syllables are all directly from the DIBELS test.)**

ful mik zum nuf kun fod vep juj sug ov wam muk lef luk lof kom
nol rez poz ol kav kic kis tek riz aj vef som zuz

"Now, do it again faster. Now faster. Now that you've picked up your speed, we will go back and read the passage we started with. Did practicing the nonsense letters help you read the passage any faster, and if it did, has it helped you understand the meaning of the text?

"When you look at the nonsense 'words' above, do you see any similarity between them and real words? If so, what are good readers—those who believe text is supposed to make sense—going to pronounce when they come to a word such as *mik* or *fod* or wam? Do you think a good reader is more likely to pronounce the nonsense syllable *mik* as *milk*? Would you yourself be more likely to pronounce the nonsense syllable som as the word some (which would be wrong) as opposed to using the short-o sound? Are readers who expect text to make sense penalized along with minority children who may read very well even though their pronunciation of nonsense syllables is hampered by their accents?

"Does DIBELS encourage students to turn good sense into *non*-sense? Does it hobble struggling readers by tangling them up in meaningless particles of language? Does it discriminate against minorities and English language learners and widen the achievement gap based on performance of nonsense?"

The Proof

There are lots of good quotes here based on the federal government's research. Furthermore, you can access Jay Samuels' entire PowerPoint slideshow for your workshops at www.reading.org/downloads/annual_handouts/j_samuels.ppt

1. **A body of scientific research shows that fluency is related to comprehension only for beginning readers (in first and second grades). In fact, after second grade, the correlation falls to near zero. Fast reading does not guarantee comprehension. That is a false assumption.**

The following quotes are from National Reading Panel contributor Steven Stahl's chapter on fluency in the federally approved book *The Voice of Evidence in Reading Research*:

"Oral reading accuracy is related to comprehension only in first and second grades with the correlations in third grade and beyond falling to near zero" (p. 190).

"Sometimes children can read accurately but do not understand what they read" (p. 188).

"Teaching children simply to say isolated words faster does not seem to improve reading comprehension. A number of studies have examined teaching children to say words . . . . faster. Although all found that children's passage reading fluency improved, NONE found differences in comprehension between the study group and the control group" (p. 189).

Note: *DIBELS training is even more fragmented than rapid word identification. Its subtests are based on rapid nonsense word/syllable "barking."*

Stahl, S. (2004). What do we know about fluency? Findings of the National Reading Panel. In P. McCardle & V. Chhabra (Eds.), *The voice of evidence in reading research* (pp. 187 – 211). Baltimore, MD: Brookes Publishing.

These next quotes are from Jay Samuels, 2006 cochair of the fluency subgroup of the National Reading Panel:

"Beware. Speed of barking at print does not inform you if students can understand the material" (slide #18).

"Many English Language Learners (ELL) can decode with speed but have poor comprehension because of vocabulary problems. These students are not fluent readers of English" (slide #19).

Samuels, S. J. (2006, May 2). *Introduction to reading fluency.* Paper presented at Spotlight on Fluency: Research and Practice from International Reading Association Publications, 51st IRA Annual Convention, Chicago, IL. PowerPoint available by going to Google and typing in: www.reading.org/downloads/annual_handouts/j_samuels.ppt

2. **DIBELS "comprehension" scores are based on the number of words in a student's retelling of a passage. It is extremely difficult to count the words. It is possible for a student to scramble words and still get a good score. The emphasis throughout is on quantity, not quality.**

Here is a quote from reading researcher Kenneth Goodman; his book, a comprehensive analysis of DIBELS, comes with a DVD containing excellent material for PowerPoint presentations:

"Strangely, the Retelling Fluency score [the comprehension subtest for DIBELS] is limited to counting the words the child used in retelling. No attention is paid in scoring to how well the retelling represents the meaning of the passage . . . . Again, as in other subtests of DIBELS, if the children are rehearsed on reading fast and saying as much as they can about each passage as fast as they can, they will improve their score on this subtest. But it would be hard to see that as progress in reading competence" (p. 31).

> Goodman, K. (Ed.). (2006). *DIBELS: What it is, what it does.* Portsmouth, NH: Heinemann.

3. **Fluency is a result of contextual reading, including sustained silent reading. It should not be practiced aside from authentic contextualized reading experiences, as with DIBELS.**

Here is a quote from the federal government's National Reading Panel:

"Competent reading requires skills that extend beyond the single word level to contextual reading, and this skill can best be acquired by practicing reading in which the words are in a meaningful context" (p. 3-13).

> National Institute of Child Health and Human Development. (2000). *The report of the National Reading Panel: Teaching children to read* (00-4769). Washington, DC: U.S. Government Printing Office.

4. **The research on the DIBELS Web site is not based on objective, independent, and reliable research. Independent research shows significant discrepancies between the claims made on the DIBELS Web site and the reality of its results.**

DIBELS training makes students better at DIBELS. The scores do not predict or help with performance on other measures of reading ability.

The following quotes are from an independent research project on DIBELS conducted by National Reading Panel contributor Michael Pressley and his team of researchers. Their objective studies found that 1) the DIBELS oral fluency measures did not result in growth in comprehension, 2) the research presented on the DIBELS Web site was conducted by people associated with DIBELS and/or Reading First, 3) there were discrepancies between the independent research findings and the DIBELS claims, and 4) DIBELS is a poor predictor of future reading success.

"[DIBELS was] produced by individuals either associated with DIBELS or Reading First" (p. 20).

"Based on available data, the fairest conclusion is that DIBELS mis-predicts reading performance on other assessments much of the time, and at best is a measure of who reads quickly without regard to whether the reader comprehends what is read. Consequently, they strongly suggest that the whole issue of validating DIBELS should be reopened before districts spend time and money on an assessment that is not a valid predictor of reading proficiency" (p. 2).

"We cannot reconcile the difference in outcome reported here and in the previous work [the research of the DIBELS associates] . . . . We think the slippage between our results and those available on the DIBELS site, all of which were produced by individuals either associated with DIBELS or Reading First, makes clear that there needs to be additional study of the DIBELS oral fluency measure by individuals not closely associated with the measure" (p. 23).

"Correlations between the Oral Reading Fluency scores and Oral Retelling scores [the DIBELS measure for comprehension] were very low" (p. 17).

Pressley, M., Hilden, K., & Shankland, R. (2005). An evaluation of end-grade-3 Dynamic Indicators of Basic Early Literacy Skills (DIBELS): Speed reading without comprehension, predicting little. East Lansing, MI: Michigan State University Literacy Achievement Research Center.

5. **DIBELS discriminates against minorities. Decisions based on DIBELS widen, rather than narrow, the achievement gap because DIBELS scores are based on a pronunciation chart. There is no special training to help teachers decide how to account for accents, dialects, and immature language.**

Here is another quote from reading researcher Kenneth Goodman:

"Since phonics is matching the patterns of English with spelling sound patterns, it is very dependent on dialect differences . . . . [For example] it is particularly likely that testers will not accept dialect and articulation responses since they would have to reconstruct how the child would have said the word . . . . Will testers accept that for some dialects row, your and more are rhyming words?" (p. 23).

> Goodman, K. (Ed.). (2006). *DIBELS: What it is, what it does.* Portsmouth, NH: Heinemann.

15
Invented Spelling

The Tough Question

My child brings home stories she's written that are full of spelling errors. She spells words the way they sound. You didn't write any corrections on her paper so she's being taught bad habits. Why not make her copy words over and over until she gets them right?

Writing

Your Bottom-Line Answer

You Can Say: Many parents and even some educators worry that children's early attempts at writing using *invented spelling*—also known as *temporary spelling* and *developmental spelling*—promote poor spelling habits. However, research reveals that the exact opposite is true. In fact, children's early explorations and discoveries about letter-to-sound relationships actually help students not just with writing, but with reading, too. It helps them gain control over all elements of language. The learning begins with meaning—the important knowledge that writing is about communicating a message. Through that quest for communication and children's struggle to figure out what letters to write, they discover a lot about language, phonemic awareness, phonics, and spelling.

If you stop and think about it, this makes sense. When a child writes "i lv dgz" instead of "I love dogs," she is actually applying sounds to letters. When she writes this way, she is thinking very hard about the connections between sounds and letters. To construct invented spellings, students form each individual sound, or *phoneme*, with their mouths. At first students actually *feel* sounds in their mouths as they apply them. As they segment and blend those sounds, they are applying what's known as *phonemic awareness*. As soon as they translate those sounds into letters on their papers, phonemic awareness becomes *phonics*—the relationship between sounds and letters. Those skills they are practicing through invented spelling—blending, segmenting, and applying sounds to letters—are all essential not just to writing, but to reading as well.

In other words, children are making meaning and practicing important skills simultaneously as they write their messages. As they construct their own spelling, children are applying what's known as the *alphabetic principle*—the knowledge that our written code connects the letters of the alphabet to sounds, and then to words, and that it all comes together to communicate a message. Through invented spelling, then, children are thinking *hard* about the basic building blocks of written language.

Even though children's early spellings are not conventional, usually their attempts do make sense, so much so that we can still make out what they're writing. Invented spelling is almost always a consistent, natural, and logical application of sounds to letters as children discover sound-to-letter connections. The mismatch is because of the irregularities of conventional spelling. It is the English print system that is the culprit, not the children.

Children learn oral language because of a need to communicate. The same is true of written language. But there are far too many such spelling irregularities for adults, much less children, to remember when they're first learning to write. As a result, children's control over oral language is often far ahead of their control over written language. The latter comes gradually over time—and only through practice. We don't help children reach the goal of control over print by discouraging practice in writing and punishing their approximations.

For example, when babies are first learning to talk, we don't force them to wait until they have mastered correct pronunciation, grammar, and vocabulary before we permit them to speak. If we did, they'd never learn to talk. Instead, we encourage their early attempts at speech. Through a lot of modeling of correct oral language, we show rather than tell them about the disconnect between their speech and standard oral language. The research confirms that children's early attempts at spelling are very similar to early attempts at speech: they're temporary and necessary developmental stages, and they should not be skipped over. And as with oral language, we urge children toward correctness by modeling standard English usage through immersion.

And so step 1—the need to communicate—leads children to step 2—discovering the letters of the alphabet they need to use in order to make their message understood. That leads to step 3—a growing recognition of spelling patterns in written English and their many irregularities. Invented spelling is also known as temporary or developmental spelling because it's only one step in a learning process leading children to conventional spelling.

Therefore, I do not insist on correct spelling when my students are first learning to write. Nor do I make them correct the words they spelled incorrectly. When I did this, I found the result was that children used only words they knew how to spell. What they wrote may have been correctly spelled, but it said nothing. So what was the point? What I sacrificed for an insistence on correct spelling was the very essence of what writing is all about. From the very beginning, I want children to realize that spelling and grammar are the tools that help us communicate. Spelling and words serve us. Both are in the service of thought and language, not vice versa.

Invented spelling is about discovery. It is not the endpoint in the writing process. It's about encouraging students to notice a vital intersection between the ideas in their heads and the letters and words that help them communicate their thoughts so others can understand them.

My job is to help children navigate yet another intersection—the intersection between where letters and sounds are consistent and where they are not. In other words, I help students to find the common ground between the consistency they expect from letters and sounds, and the erratic and random reality of standard spelling. By encouraging students to write with invented spelling, I am starting at what they know and what makes sense to them. Then I lead them toward the discovery of conventional spelling, with all its tangled combinations of randomness and consistency. This is what we do when babies are learning to talk. We start with where they are and what they know and then we help them move toward the standard conventions.

So there are two very important intersections that invented spelling helps students understand: 1) the intersection between ideas and print, and 2) the intersection between the consistencies of spelling and its irregularities. There is a common misconception that teachers who encourage students to use invented/temporary spelling don't care about correct spelling and don't care if their students care about it either. This is not true. My goal is to emphasize meaning first and to move toward a focus on conventional spelling. As a matter of fact, I use a wide variety of research-proven methods to help students learn how to spell correctly or—to use the professional term—*conventionally*:

◆   I do a lot of writing as the students watch. I encourage them to help me sound out the words as I spell them. This way, they are simultaneously seeing that writing expresses ideas and that there is sometimes a disconnect between the sounds we hear and the letters we write. I use this type of *shared writing* to write letters to the class on chart paper and to write their daily news on overheads as they watch.

◆   I use what's known as a *language experience approach*. The students dictate their thoughts to me and I write them down as they watch. Then I help them read back what I've written. This way, they are seeing how correct spelling connects to sounds and how those sounds and letters can communicate their own very important ideas and stories. It shows them that writing is not something that appears magically in books, and it's not about filling in blanks on worksheets.

◆   I use these shared texts as a canvas for teaching skills including spelling and punctuation. I go back into what we've written, and highlight or, better yet, have the students highlight tricky spelling patterns, punctuation, and grammatical structures that they need to notice. This way I'm directly and explicitly teaching basic skills. By doing so, I have combined reading, writing, listening, speaking, phonics, and spelling—just as the research recommends. Each of these language arts strengthens the others.

◆ I sometimes do a form of shared writing that is often known as *interactive writing* by omitting a word but leaving one line for every letter in that word. Next I have students "pull the words" out of their mouths, stretching out the sounds so they get a sense of the individual phonemes. Then I have a student come up and put in the correct letters on the blank lines. This really helps my class see that one sound does not always equal one letter—much less the same letter—when we are spelling conventionally. As a group, we use correction tape and help the student correct his or her invented spelling attempt on our chart paper.

◆ As research says I should, I have students write every day, and I use their own writing to teach spelling—again, starting with what they know and helping them discover what they don't know. Each week, I have students choose and circle five words in a journal or a story they've written that they're unsure of and want to know how to spell. I urge them toward selecting commonly used words instead of unusual ones. In fact, I sometimes choose two of the five words from their writing to make sure we're addressing the most common sight words and not just words that don't get used very often. I then write the five words for them, spelled correctly. These five words become the students' own spelling words. Because they help choose the words, they tend to care about learning them. Later, I go around the room as the class is writing in their journals and quietly give each child his or her little spelling test.

◆ I also write back to my students in my own sentence, using the words they misspelled. For example, if a child writes, "i lv dgs n cts" in her journal or in a story, I write back, "I love dogs and cats, too. I have a big orange cat but no dogs." Spelling is a very visual skill. By writing back to students, I provide a model of correct spelling so they see the difference between what they wrote and the conventional spelling of the words rather than a bunch of red marks that only discourage them from taking risks and writing for meaning. This is similar to what we do when children are learning to talk. At first, they confuse grammatical structures and pronunciation. For example, a young child might say, "I runned to my friend." When she makes such errors (which are brilliantly logical, by the way), we gently guide her through modeling—rather than punishment. We respond, "Oh, yes. I see that you *ran* to your friend."

- I also expand on what students write, so they can see their own thoughts both validated and extended into more complex phrases for them to read. For example, if a child writes, "I lv mi dg," I might write back, "I love my cat. I wish I had a dog, too." I connect writing with reading because research proves that each of these language arts strengthens the other.

- I give students lots of time with "eyes on text" so they see words and how the letters work. The more we read together and the more they read independently, and the more we write together and the more they write independently, the more students become familiar with spelling patterns, the purposes of punctuation and grammar, and the way our language works. Research shows that the more visual exposures students have to print, the more likely it is that their spelling will improve.

- By encouraging students' invented spelling I get an indication of where they are developmentally and how much control they have over print. I can use our shared writing activities to target the spelling patterns that students are "using but confusing." If I insist on correct spelling always, I can't help students use the words they want to use. I get writing that doesn't communicate, made up of simple, safe words.

- I never require students to copy words, much less paragraphs, for practice in spelling and handwriting. The reason is that they don't have to think at all to copy. They don't have to even know what the words are to get them down on paper. I want my students to think about text and how to make writing work for them.

The federal government's approved researchers all agree: encouraging students to practice writing with invented spelling helps them in both writing and reading because it makes them think—they must think very hard about what they want to say and what they must do to express those thoughts so another human being can understand them. That is the essence of written communication. Invented spelling is a necessary and temporary developmental step on the path to conventional spelling.

Something for You to Think and Talk About

I'm going to offer some observations here that I hope you'll think about and discuss. The first concerns students' attitudes toward spelling. I think there's a misconception out there that children don't care about spelling correctly. This may be true for some intermediate and high school students, which I'll discuss in the next question, but I don't believe it's true for younger children when they're first learning to write.

What I consistently see is that the problem isn't getting children to stop using invented spelling; it is getting them to use it in the first place because they are so focused on correctness. Young children don't know how to spell very many words. As a result, during writing time in many classrooms, especially those in which there's a big focus on accuracy, masses of students will sit waving their hands in the air, waiting for the teacher to tell them the correct spelling of a word they're stuck on, rather than writing. That frantic hand waving not only is a waste of instructional time but totally defeats the very purpose of writing. It's impossible to write with any meaningful flow by stuttering and stammering your way through print, stopping after nearly every word. The big challenge is to get students to write fluently, to get their thoughts on paper without regard to spelling, and *then* to go back and correct their errors.

Another huge roadblock to fluent writing is erasing. If children are encouraged to make corrections as they go along, we get what I call "the erasing obsession." Kids will try to fix a word as they write and madly erase until they've worn a hole in their paper! I've found it's helpful to model writing on chart paper as the students watch and show them how I reread to discover omitted words and other errors. Using carets and writing corrections over omitted words prevents a lot of holes in papers, to say nothing of valuable instructional time it saves since kids are thinking, drafting, and revising instead of obsessively erasing.

One final thought here about methods used to teach spelling. A common practice is to have students copy the words they've misspelled over and over again for practice. An associated method is to require kids to copy paragraphs or sections of text from the board. What is the purpose of requiring students to copy words or paragraphs? I suppose that it is to give students practice with spelling by drawing attention to their errors and requiring them to correct their mistakes through practice. I think copying is supposed to help with word identification and maybe handwriting, too. So if that is the dream, what, then, is the reality?

I think we need to ask if students are actively thinking about what they're doing as they copy spelling words or fill them in on worksheet blanks. Are they thinking about, noticing, or making mental notes about the spellings patterns as they copy and/or rewrite words? Can they even read the words or are they just transcribing by rote, their minds on what they're doing after school? I have seen students copy entire paragraphs from the board from the bottom up, moving right to left, totally unbeknownst to the teacher.

I once did a research study in a classroom in which the teacher required a lot of copying. When I interviewed the first-grade students in that class, not one could offer an authentic purpose for writing, such as "It communicates a message" or "We can use it to make lists." Instead they said writing was about "finishing our worksheets and getting a grade" and "drawing letters." Another answer that baffled me until I thought about it was "Writing is for making our fingers strong and getting muscles." I think the latter misconception may have stemmed from confusion over the teacher's use of the term *writing exercises*! In the mind of a first grader—exercise equals muscles.

I learned an important lesson through that research: children are still making sense out of the world, and sometimes they learn lessons that we had no idea we were teaching. As David Boulton noted in an interview with Timothy Shanahan, as teachers, we are looking down at the big picture of literacy. We're on a mountaintop and we see how skills all come together to make sense—but kids are underwater, drawing letters, filling in blanks, and strengthening their finger muscles. "Writing is about drawing letters. Writing is about filling in blanks. Writing is 'to get a good grade.' We say 'writing exercises'—they think, 'Yeah, I get it. Writing is hard. It's tiring to copy. But the payoff is we get really strong fingers, so I guess it's worth it.'"

Shanahan, T. (2006). The personal and social implications of literacy and literacy instruction. An interview with David Boulton. It is available at www.childrenofthecode.org/interviews/shanahan.htm

The Proof

The National Reading Panel did not include research on writing. It was listed as an important but "neglected" topic in their review of the research. Therefore, I can't include any definitive federal research on the topic other than the fact that the NRP report recommends invented spelling. What I've done, however, is to include the work of some National Reading Panel members and Susan Neuman, who was the assistant secretary of education when No Child Left Behind was signed into law. Her research here was released by the U.S. Department of Education to explain what scientific research findings should inform instruction for Reading First according to the law.

1. **Research shows that invented spelling benefits reading as well as writing because it helps children to think about letter-sound relationships while focusing on meaning. Research shows that students who use invented spelling write more and become better readers and spellers than students in traditional spelling programs.**

Here is a quote from Susan Neuman, former assistant secretary of education. The quote is from a U.S. Department of Education document distributed to help implement No Child Left Behind:

"Some educators may wonder whether invented spelling promotes poor spelling habits. To the contrary, studies suggest that temporary invented spelling may contribute to beginning reading (Chomsky, 1979). One study, for example, found that children benefited from using invented spelling compared to having the teacher provide correct spellings in writing (Clarke, 1988). Although children's invented spellings did not comply with correct spellings, the process encouraged them to think actively about letter-sound relations. As children engage in writing, they are learning to segment the words they wish to spell into constituent sounds . . . . Clarke (1988) compared students who were encouraged to use invented spelling with those who were not encouraged to use invented spelling in their writing during the school year. On posttests these students also scored significantly higher in spelling and reading.

"These results should also help to eliminate the fear of some parents and even teachers that children who use invented spelling become poor spellers. There is no basis in the research literature for this fear; the evidence, instead, clearly favors the use of invented spelling" (p. 6).

Neuman, S. B. (2001, November). *What research reveals: Foundations of reading instruction in preschool and primary education.* Washington, DC: United States Department of Education. I highly recommend that you get it online, at www.rmcres.com/documents/what_research_reveals.pdf

Chomsky, C. (1979). Approaching reading through invented spelling. In L. B. Resnick & P. A. Weaver (Eds.), *Theory and practice of early reading* (vol. 2), (pp. 43 – 65). Hillsdale, NJ: Erlbaum Associates.

Clarke, L. (1988). Invented versus traditional spelling in first graders' writings: Effects on learning to spell and read. *Research in the Teaching of English, 22*, 281 – 309.

Federally approved researchers Marilyn Adams and National Reading Panel member Linnea Ehri also recommend that teachers encourage invented spelling because it benefits reading, writing, and spelling skills:

Adams, M. J. (1990). *Beginning to read: Thinking and learning about print.* Cambridge, MA: MIT Press.

Ehri, L. C. (1988). Movement in word reading and spelling. In J. Mason (Ed.), *Reading and writing connections.* Needham Heights, MA: Allyn & Bacon.

2. Research shows that reading and writing and spoken language should be taught together. Each strengthens the others. Therefore, interactive demonstrations of writing such as shared writing and language experience approaches help connect the two processes as well as teach students spelling and other concepts about print.

Here are two more quotes from Susan Neuman:

"Language experience charts that let teachers demonstrate how talk can be written down provide a natural medium for children's developing word awareness in meaningful contexts. Transposing children's spoken words into written symbols through dictation provides a concrete demonstration that strings of letters between spaces are words and that not all words are the same length.

"Studies . . . . confirm the value of what many teachers have known and done for years: Teacher dictations of children's stories help develop word awareness, spelling, and the conventions of written language" (p. 8).

"Reading and writing are mutually supportive and interactive processes. Good readers tend to be good writers, and good writers tend to do well in reading" (p. 11).

Neuman, S. B. (2001, November). *What research reveals: Foundations of reading instruction in preschool and primary education.* Washington, DC: United States Department of Education.

16

Spelling, Grammar, and Punctuation for Intermediate Students

The Tough Question

" There comes a time when invented spelling stops being temporary and it stops being cute. There are eighth graders who still can't spell or use correct grammar and punctuation. My son is still spelling phonetically, as in "my frend and me whent to the moovys yestrday." This sort of horrible spelling should have been dealt with early on. It's obvious it wasn't. So what's the answer? Whatever happened to standards? "

Your Bottom-Line Answer

You Can Say: This is a highly complex question, and I'd be lying if I said there is an easy answer to it. The older students are, the harder it is to pinpoint the exact source of any problem. For example, by eighth grade, we must factor in seven years of schooling that have been experienced differently by every single student. We also have to consider each student's unique personal interests, attitudes, abilities, and relationships with at least seven different teachers.

What I can do, though, is share what years of research on spelling have shown us and then tell you how I address the complex problem of any student's failure in spelling:

◆ A research study involving more than 13,000 students showed no relationship between the amount of time devoted to spelling instruction and students' ability to spell as measured by tests involving words in sentences and composition. Dropping formal spelling instruction had no effect on students' ability to spell words either in isolation or in compositions. As a teacher, I resist this brutal fact because I want to believe that spelling instruction works, but the research proves otherwise.

◆ Spelling rules don't help, either. Students who completed an entire semester of intensive study of spelling rules could not spell any better than students who said they didn't know the rules. What's more, students who studied rules soon forgot them.

◆ Research shows that no matter what instructional methods are used, about 20 percent of the population will remain poor spellers, possibly because of a neurological glitch. Furthermore, direct spelling instruction is a questionable use of instructional time because it takes about 20 minutes of spelling work to learn only one word. Why would I spend a lot of instructional time on a skill that around 20 percent of the class cannot master anyway?

◆ However, research shows that spelling is considered to be an important skill by teachers and society as a whole, and I absolutely agree. In fact, studies suggest that regardless of the quality of the content and writing, teachers grade student work lower when it includes misspellings. For employers, poor spelling can be a deal breaker in hiring. Society generally tends to perceive poor spellers as being less intelligent than good spellers.

So, we have a real dilemma. Spelling is undeniably an important skill. Poor spellers are generally regarded as being stupid or lazy. A text that is riddled with spelling errors is usually understandable, but it is distracting and casts the writer in a negative light.

Classroom Culture and Methods to Promote Correct Spelling

My goal is to establish an environment where correct spelling and grammar are not "school skills" used to mollify me as the teacher, or something students do for a good grade. My goal is to make good spelling, grammar, and clarity of written work a question of pride for students that extends beyond the walls of the classroom into their out-of-school lives. Proofreading and correcting errors must become a habit of mind. No spelling rules or instructional methods will do any good unless my students care about spelling. Therefore, I work to help them develop what Jan Turbill calls a spelling conscience. To that end, I establish a general culture of literacy and, within that culture, use specific methods to help students with spelling:

- My students know I expect final work to be spelled correctly.

- I provide time for proofreading. I also spend time helping students identify their patterns of spelling errors.

- I explicitly tell students to write first and fix later, but stress that they *must* fix their errors and assume responsibility for them.

- I model proofreading drafts of my own writing. I show how I identify my own patterns of errors in spelling, grammar, and phrasing. I show them that proofreading serves a purpose and is a necessary part of writing. I have learned over time that modeling is not about putting up a perfect, finished product that I've written. It's about showing the process I go through and how I think when I'm editing my work.

- I make sure students have spelling dictionaries, which list the most commonly misspelled words. I also have them make their own two-column lists containing the words they know will trip them up and that they need to be careful to check. Column I is titled "Word List." Column II is titled "How I Remember to Spell It," which might include mnemonics such as remembering how to spell the word *believe* with the help of the sentence "I will bel<u>ie</u>ve you if you do not l<u>ie</u>," or that *too* means *also*, and *also* ends with an *o*.

- I make sure my students spend lots of time reading. Research shows that spelling is a highly visual skill and that every exposure to a word increases our ability to spell it. This is why many of us write out our guesses at how a word is spelled: we can often tell which guess is correct just by looking at it. I encourage my students to do this, too; Jan Turbill calls this "having a go" at the word. Accordingly, all of my students keep "Have a Go" pads at their desks.

- I don't use empty spelling exercises such as "Write your spelling words in sentences." Nor do I have students look up words in the dictionary or complete spelling workbooks. Such materials do not meet my goal of helping students develop pride in and ownership of their work. Research shows that formal, commercial spelling programs are not a good use of my instructional time. Furthermore, they are not based on authentic use of language. Therefore, they do not meet my ultimate goal of helping students care enough to develop a spelling conscience.

The bottom line is that I help students understand that there is no shame in being a poor speller but that there's no excuse for spelling poorly, either. I detoxify the disability for poor spellers while helping them accept responsibility for taking the extra step necessary to clean up their work.

My goal is to help students see spelling, correct grammar, and other skills as tools for communication, not chores they do for me, their teacher. To get to that point, students must want to be part of what literacy expert and linguist Frank Smith calls "the Literacy Club." For that to happen, they must look at good writing and say to themselves, "I *want* to do that. I *can* do that! I have something important to say. I can *be* that. I am a reader. I am a writer."

Something for You to Think and Talk About

Confronting spelling problems in older students raises questions beyond how we deal with spelling. As teachers, there is so much that we cannot control. We can't control students' innate abilities, their likes and dislikes, their attitudes toward school, or the problems they have at home. Yet all of those factors affect student achievement and test scores. And they reflect on us as teachers.

Here are some questions to consider: How do we convey to parents and to the public that we as teachers and administrators are not 100 percent responsible for student achievement, be it poor spelling or any other skill, without sounding as if we are trying to wiggle out of the work we are responsible for? How do we make students *want* to learn? How do we get them to *care* about their writing and to take pride in their work beyond the temporary fix of rewards and punishments? How do we help students to view themselves as authors, or as scientists and mathematicians, so education is not confined to school but becomes a part of them and so the term *lifelong learning* is not just a buzzword? Are we more likely to achieve those goals by engaging students and making sure they feel ownership of their work or by isolated skills instruction practiced on worksheets? These are tough questions that have no easy answers or quick fixes.

The Proof

1. **A landmark study published more than 100 years ago involving more than 13,000 students showed there is little or no relationship between the time spent on spelling instruction and spelling achievement on tests involving sentences or in compositions.**

   Rice, J. M. (1897). The futility of the spelling grind. *Forum, 23,* 163 – 72.

Note: The study was carried out at a time when students were more pliable and more likely to sit still, be quiet, and follow the rules than they are today.

2. **Dropping formal spelling instruction has no effect on students' spelling of isolated words or words in compositions.**

This finding is from a study by Oliver Cornman published in 1902. You can find more about it on Jim Trelease's Web site, where Jim has reproduced "The Reading-Spelling Connection: Krashen Looks at a Century of Spelling Research." See www.trelease-on-reading.com/spelling-krashen.html

3. **An intense semester of instruction on spelling rules had no effect on the spelling of college students. Those who had "learned" the rules did no better than students who had not. In fact, the students who were taught the rules couldn't remember them anyway.**

This finding is from a study by W. Cook published in 1912. See "The Reading-Spelling Connection: Krashen Looks at a Century of Spelling Research" at www.trelease-on-reading.com/spelling-krashen.html

4. **Each spelling word learned through direct instruction takes about 20 minutes of instructional time. Given the huge number of words students must learn to spell, this result strongly suggests that direct spelling instruction cannot do the job.**

Wilde, S. (1990). A proposal for a new spelling curriculum. *Elementary School Journal, 90,* 275 – 289.

5. **Spelling is largely a visual skill, and research shows that with each successive exposure to a word through reading, the ability to recognize and correct misspellings increases.**

See "The Reading-Spelling Connection: Krashen Looks at a Century of Spelling Research" at www.trelease-on-reading.com/spelling-krashen.html

6. **Students need to develop a "spelling conscience." We need to make correct spelling an expectation of the classroom culture through the use of "Have a Go" pads and other methods.**

Gentry, J. R. (2004). *The science of spelling.* Portsmouth, NH: Heinemann.

7. **Traditional spelling instruction requiring students to memorize words for spelling tests is ineffective and inefficient.**

The following quote is from spelling expert Sandra Wilde. Sandra has created a spelling curriculum that approaches spelling instruction in a sane, doable way. I recommend that you consider it for use in your classroom:

"Kids benefit most from thinking about how spelling works and how to use it in their writing, not memorizing lists of words."

Wilde, S. (2007). *Spelling strategies and patterns.* Portsmouth, NH: Heinemann.

8. **Formal grammar instruction and rules taught apart from context is ineffective and doesn't necessarily help writing proficiency. One of the most effective ways of learning grammar is through context. Grammar instruction must be integrated using authentic reading-writing connections.**

The quote below is by Timothy Shanahan, who is on President Bush's National Literacy Panel, was a member of the National Reading Panel, and is a federally approved government researcher:

"*Grammar is a descriptive system, language seen from the outside, so to speak. Many people, competent writers included, know little about formal grammatical rules they can say little or nothing about noun-verb agreement, the formation of tenses, and the difference between active and passive sentences*" (p. 11).

Shanahan, T. (1997). Reading-writing relationships, thematic units, inquiry learning . . . . In pursuit of effective integrated instruction. *The Reading Teacher, 51,* 12 – 19.

17

English Language Learners

The Tough Question

"*This school has lots of children who speak little or no English. You allow them to speak to you in their native languages and you even intersperse some of your teaching with non-English words. You allow them to read books that are not written in English. How can you expect to help these kids pull up our school's test scores when you let them use the crutch of their native language instead of immersing them in English only?*"

Your Bottom-Line Answer

You Can Say: Research shows that it makes no sense at all to teach students in a language they don't understand. Therefore, I use the same basic teaching approach with English language learners as I use with all my students. I start with what they know. I start with where they are. I start with what they are comfortable with and then gently lead them to what they don't know.

Research shows that if I begin with students' native language knowledge and I build on it, I help them to expand their English vocabulary. This is very basic and just makes sense. It's how we help babies learn to talk. They say a simple word (*milk*) and we build on it: *Oh, you'd like some milk*. This way, the first language is a tool that helps with English. It is not a "crutch."

Simply put, I make sure my English language learners understand what I'm saying to them. Using their native language as a base (as much as I can) helps me to do that. In other words, I make sure that the input (my teaching) is "comprehensible," to quote noted educator and expert in bilingual education Stephen Krashen. Research shows that a bilingual approach to teaching provides students with comprehensible input and helps them learn English. In fact, not surprisingly, it helps them in all areas of their education.

I work very hard to help English language learners establish a strong oral language base before I even try to teach them to read in English because federal research shows that I'm doing them harm if I teach them skills before they truly understand the language. It is entirely possible to teach non-English-speaking students to "read" words in English without their understanding a single word of what they've read. But what is the point of that? Research shows that oral language for ELLs must be developed before they are taught to read. Otherwise, all I've taught them to do is parrot words.

Therefore, I make sure that I read lots of stories to students because research shows that vocabulary is learned by all students—but especially English learners—just by listening to stories. Instead of having students fill in empty blanks on worksheets and asking them to give me one-word answers in our classroom interactions, I make sure they have opportunities to talk, to express themselves, and to *construct language for authentic purposes*. I've found that pairing English language learners with fluent English speakers helps both groups to learn and grow. I ensure frequent and varied student-to-student interactions by shuffling pairs to make sure my students gain different perspectives from their classmates.

I work hard to find the intersections between what students know and the challenges of new learning. I do this by strengthening the connections between spoken English (which students can repeat *without* understanding) and true, deep understanding of vocabulary as a base for learning the English language. Here are some of the methods I use to make sure my students have the vocabulary they need:

♦ I begin this process with the simple but respectful gesture of learning the names of my English language learners. I ask them how to pronounce their names instead of shortening or changing them to make them convenient for me.

♦ I use picture books to help students acquire vocabulary. My reading of illustrated books can also provide background and help students understand social studies and science texts that are often above their reading and their language level. The picture books help contextualize concepts and vocabulary.

♦ Our classroom is filled with multicultural literature. This not only helps students with their reading skills but, through seeing themselves represented in books, it makes them feel a part of our literate classroom culture. They know that who they are is valued, respected, and affirmed.

♦ I do a lot of reading aloud and use gestures to help my students understand word meanings as we encounter them in the story.

♦ I bring in objects (*realia*) to further support vocabulary development, and I label them in many languages. English language learners and even parents can help me with this since my vocabulary in other languages is limited.

♦ I provide picture dictionaries and word walls with illustrations of common words written in many languages. I've found that it helps to have students act out verbs as well. I also use word walls as graphic representations of academic, content area vocabulary.

♦ I draw attention to words that have similar spellings and meanings in two languages, such as *continue* in English and *continuar* in Spanish. Words with common spellings and meanings are called *cognates*. Again, I work to find common language and cultural touchstones and I lead my students from there to greater challenges.

♦ The common touchstones work both ways. I honor the language abilities of my students by asking them to teach me. I ask them for the pronunciation of vocabulary words in their own language with which I'm unfamiliar. I stumble and

English Language Learners

I'm embarrassed when I try to pronounce words in another language, but I do it anyway. It shows my students that I'm willing to try and hope they will be willing to try, too. This way, we all learn something about other languages, and our classroom is richer for it.

◆ Federal research shows that reading skills in students' native language transfer and expand reading and writing in English. I'd be remiss if I didn't capitalize on that language-rich resource in my classroom.

I avoid teaching surface skills before making sure my students have a firm language foundation. Teaching students to "read" in a language they don't understand is like building a house on quicksand. It looks good for a brief moment (as the students learn to sound out words), but pretty soon it sinks

Something for You to Think and Talk About

I look at it this way: using every single resource at our disposal to make our teaching comprehensible and accessible to students—including bilingual support—is important not only because research says so, but because it just makes good sense.

If you were dropped into a classroom in China or some other country where you were unable to speak the language, wouldn't you learn Chinese more quickly if someone there could guide and support you by using at least a few words of English to help explain new information? If I were surrounded by a language I didn't understand, with no clues, no connection at all to what I am familiar with, I know I'd be lost. And there's a good chance that I'd tune out very quickly. I might eventually learn to repeat a few words and sentences even though I had no idea what they meant—like a parrot. And unfortunately, that's what happens with many English language learners who are forced to learn to read in a language they haven't mastered yet.

Here's one more common-sense example to think about. I believe it supports the findings of the federal government's research showing that bilingual education works. When traveling in foreign countries, tourists often refer to bilingual dictionaries. Would it make any sense to look up a foreign word and find only a definition of it in the original language with no English translation? Such input would be incomprehensible, wouldn't it? English language immersion and comprehensible input through the support of bilingual explanations are not mutually exclusive.

The Proof

Many of the quotes that follow are important because they are from federal research on bilingual education. Therefore, they represent the most scientific research as sanctioned by the federal government.

1. **Encouraging language development in students' first language (bilingualism) actually strengthens their acquisition of oral and written English.**

The following quote is from the executive summary of a federally sponsored research study on language-minority children and youth. The project was conducted by the Center for Applied Linguistics under the leadership of Diane August, who was the principal investigator:

"Language-minority students who are literate in their first language are likely to be advantaged in the acquisition of English literacy. It is important to take into consideration the transferability of some literacy skills, then, when planning and providing second-language literacy instruction to students who are literate in their first language . . . . Oral proficiency and literacy in the first language can be used to facilitate literacy development in English" (p. 6).

> August, D., & Shanahan, T. (Eds.). (2006). *Developing literacy in second-language learners: Report of the national literacy panel on language-minority children and youth (executive summary).* Mahwah, NJ: Erlbaum Associates.

2. **The mastery of higher-order vocabulary and language skills in a student's first language can strengthen their comprehension skills in English.**

The quote below is also from the executive summary of the report on language-minority children and youth:

"There is clear evidence that tapping into first-language literacy can confer advantages to English-language learners. For example, there is evidence that language-minority students are able to take advantage of higher-order vocabulary skills in the first language, such as the ability to provide formal definitions and interpret metaphors, when speaking a second language" (p. 6).

August, D., & Shanahan, T. (Eds.). (2006). *Developing literacy in second-language learners: Report of the national literacy panel on language-minority children and youth (executive summary)*. Mahwah, NJ: Erlbaum Associates.

3. Common bilingual touchstones between languages can be useful in strengthening vocabulary and comprehension in second language learners.

This next quote is also from the executive summary of the report on language-minority children and youth:

"Studies also indicate students are able to take advantage of cognate relationships between their first language and English—using both oral proficiency and literacy in their first language—to understand English words, an important precursor to comprehension.

"There is limited evidence as well that cognate knowledge is associated with the development of reading comprehension in English. Cognates are words that have similar spellings and meanings in two languages, such as 'continue' in English and 'continuar' in Spanish" (p. 6).

August, D., & Shanahan, T. (Eds.). (2006). *Developing literacy in second-language learners: Report of the national literacy panel on language-minority children and youth (executive summary)*. Mahwah, NJ: Erlbaum Associates.

4. Students who do not know how to read and who do not know English should be taught to read in their native language if possible while receiving instruction in oral proficiency in English.

The following quote is from Catherine Snow, who is one of the leaders in bilingual education and is a federally approved researcher. She is citing another large federal study, published by the Committee on the Prevention of Reading Difficulties in Young Children:

"Thus, the report on preventing reading difficulties made the following recommendation concerning reading instruction for children who arrive at school not knowing English and not knowing how to read: that such children be taught to read in their native language if that is feasible (that is, if instructional materials and qualified teachers are available, and if such children are sufficient in number to justify native language reading instruction), while also receiving instruction focused on building oral proficiency in English" (p. 244).

Snow, C. E. (2000). Brookings papers on education policy: Comment by
Catherine Snow on the federal bilingual education program.
Washington, DC: Brookings Institute Press.

5. **It is possible to teach children to read in a language they do not understand, but they wind up simply parroting words, so this practice is ultimately harmful.**

Here is another quote from Catherine Snow:

"The committee report concluded that . . . . instruction that involves teaching children to read in a language they do not understand cannot constitute good instruction" (p. 245).

Snow, C. E. (2000). Brookings papers on education policy: Comment by
Catherine Snow on the federal bilingual education program.
Washington, DC: Brookings Institute Press.

6. **Our teaching (input) must be comprehensible or we're wasting our time and frustrating our students. No one learns when they're frustrated. Bilingual touchstones in language help us to achieve the goal of comprehensible input and instruction that is somewhat challenging but not frustrating, thus creating an optimal environment for English language acquisition. This is just common sense.**

The quote below is from the work of Stephen Krashen, one of the foremost authorities on bilingual education. His work is widely cited by federally approved researchers such as Catherine Snow and is commonly referred to in federal research studies:

"What theory implies, quite simply, is that language acquisition, first or second, occurs when comprehension of real messages occurs, and when the acquirer is not 'on the defensive.' . . . . Language acquisition does not require extensive use of conscious grammatical rules, and does not require tedious drill. It does not occur overnight, however. Real language acquisition develops slowly, and speaking skills emerge significantly later than listening skills, even when conditions are perfect. The best methods are therefore those that supply 'comprehensible input' in low anxiety situations, containing messages that students really want to hear" (pp. 6 - 7).

Krashen, S. D. (1981). *Principles and practice in second language acquisition,* English Language Teaching series. London: Prentice-Hall International (UK) Ltd.

18
Phonics and Second Language Acquisition

The Tough Question

" Why don't you teach more phonics and grammar to English language learners? How are they supposed to learn to read and raise the school's test scores if they don't get the basic building blocks and sounds of English? "

Your Bottom-Line Answer

You Can Say: I do teach grammar and I do teach phonics. I teach these skills through real reading and writing activities instead of in isolation. Large, federal studies of the most effective ways to teach English language learners (ELLs) have shown:

- Formal instruction of grammar and phonics that is isolated from how skills are used is ineffective, especially for English language learners.

- It is a huge mistake to teach ELLs phonics and other decoding skills before students can speak English and have a substantial vocabulary and understanding of the language. Such instruction is deceptive. Research shows that instruction focusing on phonics, decoding, and formal grammar is deceptive. ELLs *appear* to "read" as well as their native English-speaking peers until about fourth grade. From there, it becomes obvious that they cannot comprehend what they're "reading" as the material becomes more difficult. I would be doing ELLs a disservice if I taught them merely to parrot sounds rather than to think and comprehend.

Something for You to Think and Talk About

The federal government completed a large, comprehensive research study in 2006. The results of the study confirmed two main findings that advocates for bilingual education and second language learning have known for decades:

1. Bilingual education and encouraging students to read and speak in their native language help students to read, write, and acquire vocabulary in English. In other words, language skills are transferable. Furthermore, English immersion and bilingual support for students are not mutually exclusive concepts. We can immerse students in English and still support them by using their first language as a touchstone.

2. Teaching isolated skills such as phonics and spelling is worse than useless because the results are deceptive. These skills give the illusion of success because students can decode, or sound out words, but may not have the language and vocabulary base they need to comprehend the texts they can decode. Focusing on decoding and other skills without developing a language base sets students up for failure.

It is absolutely possible to teach phonics to English language learners when they don't understand the language. It is absolutely possible to teach them to sound out words even if they understand little or no English. The results look a lot like "reading." Mastery of isolated skills may enable students to identify the parts of speech on worksheets, but there is a big gap between the ability to perform isolated, surface skills and the true, deep comprehension of how those skills are used to communicate. This is true of formal, decontextualized grammar instruction too. A review of more than a hundred years of research on teaching grammar showed that there is no evidence that such instruction helps students in writing, or in any language skills for that matter.

The Proof

1. **It does no good to teach children to sound out words they don't understand, and yet many reading programs rely heavily on phonics rather than language development.**

The following quote is from "Teaching Non-native Speakers to Read," which cites the federally funded Rand Report, written by federally approved researcher Catherine Snow:

"Students who can 'read' English fluently may have only a limited understanding of the words they can decode. The findings of the Rand Report (2002) have confirmed that even for English speakers, an overemphasis on teaching discrete language skills such as decoding has stunted children's comprehension . . . .

"The differences between academic language proficiency and both conversational fluency and discrete language skills are highlighted by what is commonly termed the fourth-grade slump. The fourth-grade slump refers to the phenomenon whereby low-income students who demonstrate grade-level reading performance in the primary grades 1 – 3 begin to fall significantly behind grade norms starting at grade 4, with the discrepancy growing larger with each succeeding grade" (p. 7).

Stanley, N. (2002, August). Teaching non-native speakers to read. *Language Magazine*, 36.

Snow, C. E. (2000). Brookings papers on education policy: Comment by Catherine Snow on the federal bilingual education program. Washington, DC: Brookings Institute Press.

Rand Reading Study Group. (2002). *Reading for understanding: Toward an R&D program in reading comprehension.* Santa Monica, CA: Rand Reading Study Group.

The quotes below are from the executive summary of the report on the language-minority children and youth. The project was conducted by the Center for Applied Linguistics under the leadership of Diane August, who was the principal investigator:

"It is not enough to teach language-minority students reading skills alone. Extensive oral English development must be incorporated into successful literacy instruction. The most promising instructional practices for language-minority students bear out this point: Literacy programs that provide instructional support of oral language development in English, along with high-quality instruction in literacy skills and strategies, are the most successful . . . .

"Instruction in the key components of reading is necessary–but not sufficient–for teaching language-minority students to read and write proficiently in English. Oral proficiency in English is critical as well–but student performance suggests that it is often overlooked in instruction" (p. 4).

"An important finding that emerges from the research is that word-level skills in literacy–such as decoding, word recognition and spelling–are often taught well enough to allow language-minority students to attain levels of performance equal to those of native English speakers. However, this is not the case for text-level skills–reading comprehension and writing. Language-minority students rarely approach the same levels of proficiency in text-level skills achieved by native English speakers" (p. 4).

"Well-developed oral proficiency in English is associated with English reading comprehension skills for these students [English language learners]. Specifically, English vocabulary knowledge, listening comprehension, syntactic skills and the ability to handle metalinguistic aspects of language, such as providing definitions of words, are linked to English reading and writing proficiency" (p. 5).

"Bilingual education benefits students significantly more than English-only instruction. There is clear evidence that encouraging students to build on reading, writing, and vocabulary in their first language causes significant transfer to literacy development in English" (p. 6).

Smart Answers to Tough Questions

August, D., & Shanahan, T. (Eds.). (2006). *Developing literacy in second-language learners: Report of the national literacy panel on language-minority children and youth (executive summary)*. Mahwah, NJ: Erlbaum Associates.

2. Basic skills such as phonics and grammar should be taught in context—simultaneously with meaning through authentic text.

The following quotes are also from the executive summary of the language-minority children and youth report:

"These findings help explain why many language-minority students can keep pace with their native English-speaking peers when the instructional focus is on word-level skills, but lag behind when the instructional focus turns to reading comprehension and writing" (p. 5).

"More complex, innovative programs typically taught several of these components simultaneously—and these efforts were usually successful in improving literacy for language-minority students" (p. 4.).

"Studies that compare bilingual instruction with English-only instruction demonstrate that language minority students instructed in their native language as well as in English perform better, on average, on measures of English reading proficiency than language-minority students instructed only in English" (p. 6).

August, D., & Shanahan, T. (Eds.). (2006). *Developing literacy in second-language learners: Report of the national literacy panel on language-minority children and youth (executive summary)*. Mahwah, NJ: Erlbaum Associates.

3. Reviews of research show that formal grammar instruction is ineffective in improving students' language skills.

"A summative evaluation of a Program English curriculum . . . found that the effects of a study of transformational grammar on the language growth of secondary school students was negligible" (p. 26).

Elley, W. B., Barham, I. H., Lamb, H., & Wyllie, M. (1975). The role of grammar in a secondary school curriculum. *New Zealand Council for Educational Studies, 10,* 26 – 41.

4. A review of 100 years of research including 31 studies of formal grammar showed that teaching decontextualized English grammar in schools is a waste of time because it does not improve writing skills.

"Many young people find aspects of grammar technical and an abstraction from language itself."

Anderson, R., Torgerson, C., Beverton, S., Freeman, A., Locke, T., & Low, G. (2005). The effect of grammar teaching on writing development. *British Educational Research Journal, 32*(1), (543 – 554).

19
Terminology and Definitions

The Tough Question

" There are a lot of testing terms that I don't understand. What are percentiles, stanines, and grade equivalents, and what exactly are these 'standardized tests' that I hear so much about? "

Your Bottom-Line Answer

You Can Say: Testing terminology can be confusing, even to teachers. A test is *standardized* if it meets two criteria:

1. The test must always be administered under the same conditions. Teachers are given specific directions for what to say and what to do as they administer the tests. Sometimes these conditions are even overseen by others to make sure teachers enforce time limits and don't help or give hints to students during the test taking.

2. Each type of standardized test is scored the same way. There is no variation in how the tests are scored or how the scores are interpreted. Two people looking at the answers would score them exactly the same. Therefore, to eliminate variations and interpretations in scoring, the types of questions asked on standardized tests are restricted, as much as possible, to those that have right or wrong answers.

There are two main categories of standardized tests: *norm-referenced tests* and *criterion-referenced tests.*

Norm-Referenced Tests

These tests measure students against other students instead of assessing their individual performance or growth. The "norms" are actually a yardstick of where all the students who took the test placed. Those scores are lined up from lowest to highest and each student's score is placed along that scale.

In order to create that normed scale, student scores are referred to by terminology that describes how each student did compared to the others who took the same test. The goal of testing companies is to create tests that produce scores that form a *bell-shaped curve.* That curve has a large cluster of scores in the middle, where most students place. Then, from that middle bulge, the curve slopes downward so that the fewest scores fall at the extreme high and low ends.

That bell-shaped curve is the test makers' ideal. They manipulate their questions so that, as much as possible, a normal curve is maintained. If too many scores are clustered too high or too low, the curve becomes *skewed.* When that happens, the testing companies create new questions to get the bulk of the scores in the middle. In other words, the test is *renormed*.

Since norm-referenced tests compare students to one another, labels are assigned to how students rank. Two of the most common terms for labeling students and showing where they rank next to others are by *percentile* and *stanine*.

Stanines are one way of ranking/comparing students. In order to determine a stanine, the scores for a test are laid out from lowest to highest. Those scores are divided into nine intervals. Each of those nine intervals becomes a stanine, with one as the lowest and nine as the highest. One of the common misconceptions about stanines is that the number of scores (students) in each stanine rank is equal. However, because stanines are based on a normal distribution (bell-shaped curve), the majority of scores are clustered toward the middle. Far fewer students rank at the ends of the scale, or in the first and ninth stanines.

If you look at the table here, you'll see that the first (lowest) and the ninth (highest) stanine each represents about 4 percent of the student scores. In contrast, the middle stanine (the fifth) represents about 20 percent of the scores. This makes sense. More students are "average" than are very high or very low on most assessments.

For purposes of understanding stanines, what you need to know is that one is the lowest and nine is the highest and five is about average in terms of performance.

Result Ranking	4%	7%	12%	17%	20%	17%	12%	7%	4%
Stanine	1	2	3	4	5	6	7	8	9

Another term that sometimes confuses parents and even teachers is *percentile*. Like stanines, percentiles are a way of labeling how students performed compared to others. With percentiles, the scores are laid out and the range of scores are divided into hundredths. If a student places at the sixty-fifth percentile, this means that she scored better than 64 percent of the others who took the test. If a student scores at the ninety-ninth percentile, she did better than 98 percent of the others who took the test.

What's important to remember is that percentiles represent a student's rank compared to others. They are *not* percentages and they don't refer to the percentage of questions a student answered correctly on a given test.

Other terms that are used when discussing student scores but are less important in terms of standardization are *mean*, *median*, and *mode*. Simply put, the mean is the average of all the test scores. The scores are added and then divided by the number of students who took the test. Using the mean as a reference point can be deceptive, however. Suppose, for example, that seven students took a test with 100 points on it and the scores were as follows:

65, 66, 67, 68, 100, 100, 100

If we add the scores, we come up with 566. When we divide 566 by 7, we have an average, or mean, of 81 percent. This gives the impression that students performed pretty well on the test. However, when we look at the scores, we see that more than half the students failed and the 81 percent is deceptive.

The median is the point that is midway among the scores when they are laid out in a line from lowest to highest. In the distribution above, the median is 68 because half the scores are above it and half the scores are below it. If there are an even number of scores, then the median is the number halfway between the middle two scores.

The mode is the score that occurs most frequently. In the distribution above, the mode is 100. Again, this can be a somewhat confusing or even deceptive way to describe the test results because it gives the impression that overall the students performed better on the test than they actually did. If someone wanted to paint a rosy picture, they could report the mode of this particular distribution. On the other hand, if someone wanted the school or the teachers to look bad, he could report the median, 68.

Both statements are technically true. But both are deceptive and neither gives an honest, complete picture of student performance.

The point is that the reporting of test scores can be manipulated, and we need to be wary of deceptive representations. The same can be said of reporting of statistics.

Whoever reports the data can cherry-pick—be selective—and manipulate the findings without actually out-and-out lying. Therefore, we shouldn't assume that data, test scores, and other statistics we read in the paper or hear reported on the news are necessarily accurate. Whoever reports the story can make schools and teachers look good or bad depending on how she decides to organize the data.

Two other terms that are associated with tests are *validity* and *reliability*. Both are essential to the integrity of the testing process. Without them, we might as well forget it. *Validity* refers to the content of the test and whether it actually assesses what it claims to be assessing. For example, are the questions on standardized achievement tests true representations of what students have achieved? If the questions are narrow (selected to test a few obscure or unnecessary concepts), then the test is not really a valid measure of achievement. If a test claims to assess mathematical achievement but tests only students' knowledge of addition and multiplication tables and not their ability to problem solve, then the test is probably not valid. Similarly, if a student excels in mathematical problem solving but has a reading problem and can't read the questions on the test, then the test is in part assessing reading ability and would not be a valid measure of that student's ability in mathematics.

The same questions arise concerning assessments of reading ability. If an assessment is heavily weighted toward phonics and other discrete skills but claims to be measuring "reading growth," then the test is not valid because reading is more than just skills and must result in comprehension of text. If a student is anxious and is not a good test taker, then the test is not valid for that particular student because it is not a true measure of the student's achievement. This brings us to another closely related factor in testing terminology, *reliability.*

Reliability is another essential element in assessment. It refers to the consistency of a test score. Is the score a fluke, or could we expect a student to perform at about the same level of proficiency if she were to take the test at another time? Reliability is affected by a number of factors. If a student is ill at the time of the test, or her dog just died that morning, or she just moved to a new school after losing her home and family members in Hurricane Katrina—then the score is not reliable. On another day, under better circumstances, the score could be radically different. Obviously, reliability and validity are closely related.

In summary then, standardized tests that compare students to one another are norm-referenced tests.

Criterion-Referenced Tests

The second type of standardized test is the *criterion-referenced test.* Like norm-referenced tests, criterion-referenced assessments *may* be standardized (given under consistent conditions, using the same questions and directions, and scored uniformly, without bias or interpretation). However, instead of comparing students to one another, criterion-referenced tests compare students to a predetermined standard of performance. Scores are reported as percentages, or number correct, rather than by percentiles and stanines. Students, then, must reach a certain target, or *benchmark*, in order to pass.

The same questions about reliability and validity that apply to norm-referenced tests also apply to criterion-referenced standardized tests. Are the standards and benchmarks valid measures of what students need to know? Are the assessments reliable? Are the stakes too high to be determined by a single test score based on the test makers' notions about what students need to know and how they need to demonstrate that knowledge?

Something for You to Think and Talk About

A lot depends on standardized test scores. They impact students' futures, what curriculum can be used in schools, how much the federal government can intrude into our classrooms, whether or not schools stay open or are shut down, and even whether administrators and teachers keep their jobs. The something to think about is this: Teachers are overwhelmed by day-to-day struggles at the classroom level. It's difficult to juggle even one more tiny ball, much less to keep track of the political ramifications of testing and other issues that loom large in the media and the minds of parents.

What I'm suggesting, though, is that we teachers need to be informed and to keep track of how the data is manipulated and how we and our schools are held 100 percent accountable for student performance. We must not fall into the trap of assuming that tests are the ultimate author on students' abilities and our effectiveness as teachers. Tests, like the human beings who construct them, are fallible.

The Proof

In self-defense, we teachers need to address attacks on schools and defend students and good practice. Since we are overworked and overwhelmed as it is, at the end of the next section, beginning on page 153, I suggest some Web sites you can visit to help unravel the complex issues we face, along with the quotes and the references for this question on testing and accountability. Of course, I hope this book will help, too!

20

Problems With and Inequities in High-Stakes Testing

The Tough Question

Teachers are always complaining about standards and testing. How can our children succeed without high standards? Why are you so afraid of being held accountable?

Your Bottom-Line Answer

You Can Say: I am not opposed to testing, standards, or being held accountable for the quality of my teaching. However, I am opposed to testing that penalizes or rewards students on the basis of a single test score. Often a single score on one of these *high-stakes tests* determines if your child will be promoted to the next grade or retained, or whether she will graduate from high school. I am opposed to the misuse and abuse of high-stakes testing because those tests don't help me help your child. There are many problems with high-stakes tests that can make them harmful to schools:

- The tests we give to satisfy federal regulations are standardized and based on "norms." This means they compare your child to other children across the country. They are not based on the individual growth of your child. Whether or not your child improves from one year to the next is irrelevant on these tests. In fact, whether or not a school improves from year to year is largely irrelevant. Success or failure is based on how your child or your child's school does compared to other students or other schools.

- The standardized achievement tests are based on a system that makes sure some children and some schools lose. In fact, if too many students begin to do well on a test, the companies change it to make sure a prescribed number of students fail or at least score "below average." If all students in the country increased their scores so they were at the top 10 percent of the present scale, the test publishers would renorm the scale. I am not opposed to high standards, but the standards keep moving to make sure some students fail no matter how much progress they make or how well we teach. I don't see how this helps students. I want all of my students to have a chance at success.

  Imagine a horse race with ten entries. It's impossible that all ten horses will come in first. It can't happen. Half of them will finish more slowly than the average time. Even if we train those horses and they all do better than they did when they were first tested—only one can come in first and all the rest are left behind and half *must* be "below average." So, the "average" score moves up all right, but you cannot have more than half of any group above average. Failure is literally built right into the system.

- Standardized, high-stakes tests are given at the end of the school year. We don't get the results back until the following year. Therefore, the scores come back too late to inform our teaching since we now have an entirely different group of students—with different abilities and different needs—than those who took the test.

- The stakes are high for students. Important decisions about their future are made on the basis of their test results, often a single score. If your child is a poor test taker, or freezes under pressure, or is ill, it doesn't matter. Even students who have lost their homes and are displaced because their previous schools were destroyed by a hurricane must take the tests and suffer the consequences of getting a potentially lower score. That is unfair.

- Students are put under enormous pressure because of the tests. During testing time, all other activities in many schools stop. Many students become physically ill because of the pressure. We share a common goal. We both want your child to be well adjusted and happy, not sick, afraid, limited in what she is permitted to learn—and hating school.

- The stakes are high for schools as well. Schools are penalized if they don't hit certain target scores. What makes this unfair is that all schools do not have equal facilities. Some are poor, and conditions may even be unsafe. Some schools are wealthy and students have every advantage. However, regardless of the facilities and opportunities, and regardless of how far behind schools were to begin with, all are expected to meet the same testing targets in the same time frame.

- Standardized tests treat all students as if they have equal education and language backgrounds. They discriminate against English language learners. Children who have been in the country only for a year and who still have not mastered English are forced to take the tests in English. Thus, children are penalized and are labeled as "stupid" some times and schools with high minority populations are labeled as "failing" and are even closed because of low test scores.

- The tests themselves and the scoring can be flawed. Nevertheless, the scores are treated as absolutes.

- Because so much emphasis is placed on testing and because so much is at stake, we are forced to "teach to the tests." We are forced to conform to what some group of test makers for some publisher somewhere has decided is important. As a result, we eliminate many areas of the curriculum to focus on what the tests will ask. So instead of a broad, rich curriculum, our teaching becomes narrow.

- Research shows that intensive test preparation improves student performance on that particular, narrow test. However, that performance does not transfer to other important tests such as the SATs because the knowledge base has been limited by too much focus on one narrow test.

◆ Students are deprived of a lot of knowledge that does not make it onto the tests. Too much emphasis on too much testing limits your child's education.

Standardized tests are unforgiving. There is no court of appeal because the testing culture is cold, remote, and faceless. Our American values teach us the importance of individuality and compassion. The testing culture is impersonal and dispassionate. Compassion is personal. Standardization is not.

I view your child as more than a single test score. The type of assessment I prefer to high-stakes testing is called *formative assessment*. It is ongoing and specific to your child's needs. I also administer *criterion-referenced tests* that show me whether or not your child has mastered specific skills. For example, I can test to see whether your student has mastered math facts, but more important, I can test her ability to use those facts to reason and think through problems.

I compare your child's growth to her own previous performance, not to other students' progress. Whereas the scores from high-stakes standardized tests are virtually useless, as a result of formative assessment, I can change the focus of my instruction so that it is specifically tailored to my students' unique needs. This takes a lot of time on my part, but it is worth the effort. I see individualizing my instruction based on ongoing formative assessment as part of my mission as a teacher.

Something for You to Think and Talk About

I think the enormous weight given to standardized tests raises important questions about balance and about values. Somehow the whole testing movement has become a runaway train. Instead of offering us informed guidelines and reasonable, achievable standards, as well as a general yardstick to assess how well school curricula are implemented, the tests have, in fact, become the curriculum and subsequently narrowed and redefined knowledge based on arbitrary and even inaccurate guesses as to what students should know. The tail is wagging the dog.

There's another troubling consequence of high-stakes testing. In schools, we see the role of the teacher becoming increasingly distanced from the curriculum and the decision-making process. In many schools, teachers are confined to scripted or highly structured programs that run counter to the recommendations of federal research. High-stakes testing is yet another wedge between teachers and the curriculum and, worse, between teachers and students.

There is another sad truth to face here. When so much emphasis is placed on test scores, when the very jobs of teachers depend on those scores, teachers necessarily view their students differently. Instead of seeing struggling students as needing our help, I believe we are forced into a position of seeing them as burdens, or even enemies to our performance. The scores come to be the goal, the prize, the brass ring. Struggling students become obstacles to that goal. That is a shattering shift in values.

In fact, the whole school culture has undergone a shift as a result of the testing obsession that is reflected not only in the time we devote to assessments but in our language as well. For example, those students who are on the cusp and who have the greatest potential for raising schools' scores are referred to as "bubble kids" or "in the strike zone." These are the students toward whom teachers are directed to focus their attention because these are the ones who will raise schools' scores. And the others? The current mindset is to let them go.

Since the focus is to raise the scores, the kids have become by-products of that goal. Sadly, those below the "strike zone" are viewed as expendable and become collateral damage. It hurts to write these words, and it probably hurts to read them, too, but it's true. The performance obsession eclipses our ethical and moral imperative to help all children and to make *them*—not schoolwide performance—our focal point.

Another unpleasant observation here: Frequently, the language that reflects and promotes the testing culture is not just glib and depersonalized, as in the case of "bubble kids," but has assumed a distinctly military cast. For example, some programs no longer recommend building background knowledge or scaffolding or supporting students. Instead, the term is *front-loading*, which sounds like something we should be doing to a cannon rather than to children's minds. The intensive test prep time is referred to in some schools as *boot camp*. This leads to a further blurring of the military, school, and testing cultures. Such language is cold. It is dehumanizing. I don't think the use of such language is a trivial point. We are, after all, educators talking about children! I believe such language encourages teachers to define students in terms of their utility to *us* instead of asking, "What is our responsibility as a society to *them*?"

The Proof

1. Even test manufacturers themselves warn that important decisions should not be made on the basis of standardized tests.

"In embracing standardized testing as the tool of scientific measurement, they have disregarded the testers' own cautions. [Test] manuals warn that a major 'misuse of standardized achievement test scores is making promotion and retention decisions for individual students solely on the basis of these scores.'"

Winerip, M. (2003, July 23). Rigidity in Florida and the results. *New York Times*, p. B9. You can also access this article by going to www.susanohanian.org.

2. An overemphasis on test preparation narrows the curriculum and does not translate to performance on other assessments such as the SATs and NAEP scores.

Amrein, A., and Berliner, D. (2002, March 28). High-stakes testing, uncertainty, and student learning. Available at Education Policy Analysis Archives 10(18): http://epaa.asu.edu/epaa/v10n18/

3. There are numerous examples of errors in the scoring of tests. As a result, many students have been unfairly penalized. For example:

"One of the major corporations that runs the testing industry, CTB/McGraw-Hill, admitted that it had incorrectly scored the reading and math tests of nearly 10,000 students in New York City. The error made it look as if test scores had dropped precipitously from the year before. As a result, through no fault of their own, thousands of third and sixth graders were sent to summer school. So taxpayers lost money, kids lost their summer, and a number of school administrators were fired."

Goodnough, A. (2002, September 28). After disputes on scoring, school system switches provider of reading tests. *New York Times*, p. B3.

For a comprehensive examination of the dangers of standardized testing, see Alfie Kohn's seminal book on the subject:

Kohn, A. (2000). *The case against standardized testing: Raising the scores and ruining the schools?* Portsmouth, NH: Heinemann.

For a handy little pocket book explaining testing terminology, see Sandra Wilde's book:

> Wilde, S. (2002). *Testing and standards: A brief encyclopedia.* Portsmouth, NH: Heinemann.

I also highly recommend the work of Gerald Bracey. He has an amazing book that takes readers behind the curtain of research, testing, and statistical manipulations. It's highly readable and has examples you can use for workshops or in explanations in newsletters:

> Bracey, G. (2006). *Reading educational research: How to avoid getting statistically snookered.* Portsmouth, NH: Heinemann.

The following Web sites are wonderful sources for information about testing and other vital issues in education. They are clearinghouses for helping you stay informed:

www.sdkrashen.com You can go to Steve Krashen's Web site for easy-to-read explanations of how the NAEP and other test scores are manipulated. His articles deconstruct the media and federal spin. Steve saves us the hassle of deciphering all the data ourselves and guides us through the smoke and mirrors.

www.susanohanian.org Susan Ohanian's Web site is a remarkable clearinghouse for all the latest news in education—those issues that impact the lives of every teacher and every student in this country.

www.fairtest.org This site is dedicated to all issues related to testing and how they affect students, teachers, and schools. It is an eye-opener.

www.trelease-on-reading.com Jim Trelease is, of course, a cultural icon in the world of reading. His Web site is not just informative, it's colorful, teacher-friendly, and appealing, too. It is a wonderful blend of practical suggestions, ideas, and comments on literacy as well as a clearinghouse for many important literacy issues, including spelling and independent reading. His site also addresses relevant political issues such as the news and comments on federal legislation, censorship, and testing.

What Is the Role of the Teacher in Teaching?

Dear Teachers,

I almost called this section "What Is the Role of the Teacher?" instead of "What Is the Role of the Teacher in Teaching?" because the latter sounds self-evident and redundant. After all, the role of the teacher is to teach. However, the role of the teacher is not as obvious in the current educational climate as it should be.

Recently, we've seen publishers of commercial programs resurrect terms that I thought had died during the 1960s, such as "teacher-proof materials." One publisher of a prominent commercial reading series is touting its product as being so basic, and requiring so little creative effort and thought, that "anyone, even the bus driver could walk in and teach it." Instead of being a toolbox or a support mechanism for beginning teachers, the reading series *becomes* the curriculum. And when the commercial program is so scripted and so restrictive that it *is* the curriculum, it also *replaces* the teacher.

When anyone can teach, the system doesn't need you. The irony is that publishers tout their commercial programs as being based on the federal government's scientific research. This book clearly illustrates that this is not so. The vast majority of the research I cite here is from large, federally funded studies or from studies conducted by panelists and researchers who are sanctioned by the federal government. I also cite documents written by and distributed through the Department of Education to help teachers comply with No Child Left Behind. In a few cases I refer to studies that were cited in the federal research as being a force behind current legislation. Therefore, the research base in this book is unassailable. It's scientific and has been sanctioned and even funded by the federal government.

Across the board, the research shows that teachers belong not just at the physical center of the classroom, but at the scholarly and creative center as well. No research supports supplanting you with a commercial program or a scripted manual. If you can find the scientific, federal research that does that, send it to me and I'll eat it without salt.

What shines through every research-based recommendation and quote in this book, nestled between every single line, is that you are the head and you are the heart of the classroom. And now, you have the research base to assert your role, your responsibility, and your mission as a teacher of children.

Elaine Garan

Index

A

abridged stories. See commercial reading programs and guided reading
Accelerated Reader program (AR), problems with, 59–65
achievement gap, the, 19, 110, 113, 117, 146, 147
Adams, M. J., *Beginning to Read*, 73, 82, 120
administrators, notes to, 11–12, 17, 20, 57–58, 64, 66, 90–92, 93, 105–106, 123
Allington, R., & Woodside-Jiron, H., "Decodable Text in Beginning Reading," 99–100
alphabetic principle, the, 26, 30–31
  fingerpointing and, 34–36
  invented spelling and, 112
Amrein, A., & Berliner, D., "High-Stakes Testing, Uncertainty, and Student Learning," 154
Anderson, R., Torgerson, C., Beverton, S., Freeman, A., Locke, T., & Low, G., "The Effect of Grammar Teaching on Writing Development," 142
anthology. See commercial reading programs and guided reading
Applied Linguistics, Center for, 133, 140
Atwell, N., *The Reading Zone*, 55
August, D., & Shanahan, T., (Eds.), "Developing Literacy in Second-Language Learners," 133–134, 140–141

B

"barking at print," 103
basal readers. See commercial reading programs and guided reading
"bell-shaped curve" in testing, 144
"benchmarks" in testing, 148
Berliner, D. C., "Academic Learning Time and Reading Achievement," 56
big books and enlarged text
  bottom-line answer, your, 26–27
  proof, the, 29–32
  something for you to think and talk about, 27–29
  tough question, the, 25
bilingual education, 130–136, 138
  "book flood" studies, 57–58
  "book sells," 53

book walk, 46
"boot camp," as test preparation, 153
boredom, caused by
  decodable text, 98
  round-robin reading, 22, 23
  worksheets, 38, 41
Bracey, G., *Reading Educational Research*, 155
"bubble kids," 153

C

Chomsky, C., "Approaching Reading Through Invented Spelling," *Theory and Practice of Early Reading*, 119
Clarke, L., "Invented Versus Traditional Spelling in First Graders' Writings," 119–120
Clay, M. M., 50
Clay, M. M., *Reading: The Patterning of Complex Behavior*, 36
Clay, M. M., *Reading Recovery*, 95
Clymer, T., "The Utility of Phonic Generalizations in the Primary Grades," 72–73
cognates, 131
Cole, A., *When Reading Begins*, 35, 36
commercial reading programs and guided reading bottom-line answer, your, 44–47
  proof, the, 48–51
  something for you to think and talk about, 47–48
  tough question, the, 43
commercial reading programs, 40–41
comprehension
  increasing through reading aloud, 14
  through big books and enlarged text, 27
"conscience, spelling," 125, 127
constructing language, 47
consumables. See commercial reading programs and guided reading
context, learning word meanings through, 17
conventional spelling, 114
Cook, W., 126
Cornman, O., 126
Cowley, J., *Mrs. Wishy-Washy*, 35
criterion-referenced tests, 147–148, 152
cross-checking word meanings for accuracy, 93, 95
cueing systems
  graphophonemic, 90–92, 94
  semantics, 90–91, 94

  syntactic, 90–91, 92, 94
  triangulation, 90, 93
cueing systems and eye-movement research
  bottom-line answer, your, 90–92
  proof, the, 93–95
  something for you to think and talk about, 92–93
  tough question, the, 89
"culture of literacy," 124

D

daily letter, using to help students read, 28
decodable text
  bottom-line answer, your, 97–98
  proof, the, 99–100
  something for you to think and talk about, 98–99
  tough question, the, 96
decoding
  through reading aloud, 14
  through shared reading, 30–31
developmental spelling. See invented spelling
dialects, accents' interference with phonics instruction, 73, 74, 81, 110, 118
Dickinson, D. K., & Smith, M. W., "Long-term Effects of Preschool . . . ," 19
direct instruction, to teach vocabulary, 46
directionality, 26
Duckett, P., "New Insights: Eye Fixations and the Reading Process," 93
Durkin, D., *Children Who Read Early*, 20, 29–30
DIBELS (Dynamic Indicators of Basic Literacy). See fluency and comprehension/DIBELS

E

Ehri, L. C., & Sweet, J. S., "Fingerpoint Reading of Memorized Text," 36
Ehri, L. C., "Movement in Word Reading and Spelling," 120
Ehri, C., "National Reading Panel Report: Work Praised, but Distortion Fears Persist." (Interview) 82
Elley, W., 53
Elley, W., & Mangubhai, F., "Impact of Reading on Second Language Learning, The," 30, 57–58
Elley, W., "Acquiring

Literacy in a Second Language," 30, 57–58
Elley, W., Lamb, I. H., Wyllie, M., "The Role of Grammar in a Secondary School Curriculum," 141–142
Elley, W., "Vocabulary Acquisition from Listening to Stories," 16–17, 19
English language learners (ELLs)
  bottom-line answer, your, 130–132
  fluency and comprehension/DIBELS, 103, 107–108
  phonics instruction for older students, problems with, 77
  proof, the, 133–136
  something for you to think and talk about, 132
  sustained silent reading, 54
  tough question, the, 129
  value of reading aloud for, 14
  See also phonics and second language acquisition, 137–142
"erasing obsession, the," 117
excerpts. See commercial reading programs and guided reading
"eyes on text," 56
  invented spelling, 116
  phonics for older students, 77
  round-robin reading, problems with, 22

F

federal government research
  big books and enlarged text, 29–30
  commercial reading programs, 44–51
  English language learners, 130–132, 133–136
  fingerpointing, 34
  fluency and comprehension/DIBELS, 102, 106–110
  invented spelling, 116
  phonics and second language acquisition, 138–139
  phonics for older students, 77–78
  reading aloud to students, 16–17
  responsibility for knowing, 9–10
  round-robin reading, problems with, 22, 23–24
  sustained silent reading (SSR), 56–57
fingerpointing, voicepointing, and headpointing
  bottom-line answer, your, 34
  proof, the, 36
  something for you to think and talk about, 35–36